Jade Pearls and Alien Eyeballs
Unusual Edible Plants and the People Who Grow Them

Emma Cooper

Temperate Tomes

First published in Great Britain in 2014 by Temperate Tomes, 28 Pickersleigh Avenue, Malvern, WR14 2LR.

Photography, illustration, design and typesetting by Emma Cooper.

A catalogue record for this book is available from the British Library.

ISBN 978-0-9928586-1-2

About the author

By day, Emma Cooper lives the life of a science writer, helping to make science fun and accessible to the widest possible audience. By night she dons her pith helmet and explores the world of edible plants. When she finds something exciting she shares it with the world via her blog and podcast, but very occasionally she disseminates a wealth of information in book form.

'Growing Vegetables is Fun' is a magbook (or bookazine), first published by Dennis Publishing in 2008 and now on its third edition. It encourages kids of all ages to get their hands dirty and grow some of their own food, and has plenty of space for making notes and drawing pictures. It came with free seeds, but they're probably not worth sowing now.

'The Alternative Kitchen Garden: An A to Z' was published by Permanent Publications in 2009, and is the story of Emma's first garden - home to the wild and wacky, edible and useful, wonderful world of plants. It charts Emma's burgeoning compost obsession, and introduces a small flock of much-loved chickens, who are sorely missed now they've left for the big chicken coop in the sky.

'The Allotment Pocket Bible', published by Crimson Publishing in 2011, is a handy guide to taming an allotment and growing your own in a community environment. It's mainly about familiar edible plants, but encourages readers to step off the beaten track and explore the world of plants a bit further in places.

In 'The Peat-Free Diet' Emma explains how to go about gardening without using peat, whether you're a novice gardener or an old hand trying to get to grips with peat-free compost. It contains a lot of interesting stuff about seed germination, has a foreword by Alys Fowler and is available as an audiobook so you can listen while you're working in the garden.

You can find out more about each of this titles via
http://emmacooper.org/

Here be dragons

When you step off the garden path and enter the world of unusual edibles, there are risks and dangers aplenty. Toxic plants, invasive plants and even exploding plants.

No guidebook can be comprehensive about the risks (or the joys) associated with the plants. Please heed the warnings in the reference section at the end of the book and remember to do your homework.

Whilst every effort has been made to ensure the accuracy of the information included in this book, neither the publisher nor the author and contributors can take any responsibility or liability for what happens when you use it. We just hope it's fun.

Connect with Emma

On Twitter: @emmathegardener

On Facebook: https://www.facebook.com/emmathegardener

Via her website: http://emmacooper.org

CONTENTS

Preface

We live in an instant gratification society, but you can't rush a garden. The seasons turn at their own pace, and the plants respond. You may choose to force your rhubarb (or your sea kale!), or grow near-instant microgreens on your windowsill, but if there's one thing a garden will teach you, it's patience.

I first started collecting the stories of the modern day plant hunters featured in this book in the summer of 2010. Since then the manuscript has been put on hold more than once, disappearing from view for months on end. But, like a bulb under the winter soil, it was merely dormant and not dead.

I would like to thank all of those who have added their stories to the book, and those who have supported me during its periods of growth and torpor. Special thanks go to Owen Smith, whose red pen removed all kinds of errors and inaccuracies from the draft manuscript. Any that remain, of course, are entirely down to me.

Every journey begins with a single step. This one begins within the thought that you might like to *grow something different* in the kitchen garden this year. A guidebook of sorts, Jade Pearls and Alien Eyeballs offers you stories from travellers who have stood where you stand, and who have seen and grown the plants you may choose to grow and eat. But there is no map, and if you choose to walk this path then your own personal garden of unusual delights will be truly unique.

I hope you enjoy the book, and the journey, and that you'll choose to send the occasional postcard to your fellow plant hunters.

Bon voyage!

Emma cooper, Oxfordshire, March 2014

Emma Cooper

Introduction

Edible plants can be exotic, old-fashioned, wild or just plain weird. Think of the things you consider to be unusual – things you've seen in the produce section, or the latest 'superfruit' to be mentioned in the media. Perhaps you encountered something new on holiday, and wished you could bring it home with you. Your list would be different from my list, which would be different from everyone else's, because what counts as unusual depends on both your past experiences, where you live and when you live – there are trends and fashions in food and horticulture, as in anything else.

An unusual plant may have been commonly grown in the past, or it may have been bred only recently and be something truly new. Or it may come from far away (a concept that still exists, even with globalisation). It may be a plant that is very commonly grown and known in agriculture, but not often cultivated at home - or the reverse, a plant that is common in gardens and on allotments but rarely commercially available.

My personal choice is to define an unusual edible plant as one that you wouldn't easily find (or would pay a fortune for) as a food product, or one that's not commonly on sale at your local garden centre or plant nursery. Only a small proportion of those plants can make it onto these pages, but I hope they serve to whet your appetite for searching out and growing your own.

Why would people want to step off the beaten garden path and grow something unusual? At the simplest level, I think there is a natural human impulse to seek out new and interesting things, to collect them, to experience them, and for gardeners to grow something new just to see if they can.

But beyond that people have some very serious reasons why they decide to grow their own food, and why they go beyond that to grow edible things that are unusual. Growing your own food (even on a tiny scale), harvesting it and then serving and eating it, is a profound experience that many people find so rewarding it is almost addictive. That is certainly my experience – I started growing a few herbs and leafy greens in pots on my patio and fell in love with the plants themselves and the sheer joy of eating things that I had grown. I want to see them all, to know them all, an impulse that still drives me now – the better part of a decade later – even though I now know that such a thing would be impossible.

One of the big motivations behind growing unusual edibles is concern at the state of our planet and what our current forms of agriculture and horticulture are doing to it. Many of our favourite food crops are grown in environmentally-damaging ways, with heavy use of water for irrigation, or chemical pesticides and fertilisers that leave residues in our food and ultimately in us. Modern plant varieties are bred to be grown in monocultures – huge, otherwise sterile fields – and to rely on these inputs. The crop matures all at once, and is bred for long shelf-life and the ability to withstand transportation and handling, and to look perfect on the shelf. Flavour, diversity and resilience are not in the mix.

And so there are people who are trying to do things differently. Some are growing unusual edible plants because they want to preserve heritage and heirloom varieties that are in danger of being lost – varieties that were bred over generations to provide food plants that thrive in particular conditions, taste good, store well or ripen over long periods of time to allow continuous harvests.

Some people are growing these plants because they haven't been bred to expect the high inputs of the commercial agricultural system and thrive without chemical inputs and so are chemical-free when they arrive on your plate. Others are growing them this way as part of sustainable, low-input systems and are developing techniques that will help our gardens remain productive in our changing climate and when our supplies of oil run out. Increasing the genetic diversity of our food crops, and the variety of plants we grow, increases our resilience – in the event that one crop fails in a season, there are others to harvest.

There are others who garden this way as a political act, refusing to buy products from agribusiness, to have their food choices dictated to them, and to be part of such a damaging system. Others simply find them beautiful, and love their contribution to a flourishing, scented garden that is bursting with other forms of life as part of as complete an ecosystem as possible.

Throughout this book you will find profiles of people who grow unusual plants. Some of them do it for a living, and others are keen amateurs who fit these wonderful plants into often hectic lives. You can hear, in their own words, why doing so is important to them.

I started growing a few edible plants on the patio when I moved into my first house, because I was developing an interest in the environment and I was concerned about food miles. Mint, lettuce, beetroot, garlic and potatoes all grew happily in containers. Alongside them was a pot of leaf beet - a leafy vegetable that's almost never sold. I bought seeds for it at the local DIY store, attracted by its potential as a stir-fry vegetable. It's a smaller version of chard, without the thick and colourful stems, and it has become a firm favourite in my garden. I also dabbled in coriander, a leafy herb that's very useful for Indian and Mexican cooking (also known as cilantro). Coriander has a tendency to bolt (flower and set seed at an alarming rate), but the seeds are used as a spice.

As my garden grew I joined Garden Organic (the HDRA as it was known then) and signed up for their Heritage Seed Library (HSL). The HSL is conserving heritage or heirloom varieties of seed - varieties that are no longer commercially available. They also stock the occasional oddity, and it was from them that I received my first achocha seeds. Achocha is one of the Lost Crops of the Incas, a fruiting vegetable that is related to cucumbers and melons and which is still grown in its native South America but that never really caught on elsewhere in the world. Now that there is increasing interest in growing unusual edibles, achocha seeds are quite easy to get hold of (although it's still nearly impossible to buy achocha fruit), and attention has moved on to other South

American crops such as yacón, ulluco, mashua and oca.

My list of new plants for 2010 (not all of which made it into the garden) included oats, feverfew, Opium poppies, golden hop, aronia, capers, luffa, saffron and crimson-flowered broad beans. In 2011 I didn't have much luck with chayote, but had great success with stevia grown from seed.

I added a lot of fruit plants to the garden, and my attention is turning towards more perennial plants - I love the forest garden concept. The list of plants I want to grow is growing ever longer, and I have to prune the list down every year to something manageable that will fit in the available space.

My seeds and plants come from a wide variety of sources, including popular online seed suppliers, independent concerns, seed swaps and more personal exchanges. I love Real Seeds, as much for their ethos as the contents of their catalogue. You'll find a list of suppliers at the end of the book, and plenty of advice on sourcing plants as we go along.

I have a small army of books and websites I refer to in my search for information, and you'll find some of those listed at the end of the book as well. For now I will simply say that I have been blogging and podcasting about my forays into adventurous gardening since the beginning - have a look at my website (http://emmacooper.org). After the first five years or so I wrote a book (The Alternative Kitchen Garden: An A to Z, published by Permanent Publications) that details my successes and failures with common and unusual edibles, as well as some of the ways in which environmental issues and gardening interact.

CHAPTER ONE

Historical Unusual Edibles

A potted history of plant hunters

From the moment we developed agriculture we seem to have developed an insatiable curiosity about new plants - perhaps it is an adaptation of the hunter-gatherer mindset. Certainly there have been plant-hunting expeditions throughout history. The first one recorded was commissioned by Queen Hatshepsut of Egypt, in the 15th century BC, to collect incense trees (several species that produced aromatic resin) from Punt (although it's not entirely clear where Punt was).

Alexander the Great was encouraged to take botanists on his conquering expeditions, and to send samples of potentially useful new plants back home. And the Romans took their favourites with them wherever they went, introducing to Britain such useful plants as walnuts, figs, leeks, alexanders, sweet chestnuts and the opium poppy.

From the 8th to 15th centuries, Islamic conquerors of the countries bordering the Mediterranean brought new crops from India and the Far East, including lemons and limes, apricots, bananas, rice, taro and sugar cane.

And in the 15th century, changes to the political landscape caused disruption to the supplies of spices that Europe had come to depend upon, and which were a considerable source of wealth. This prompted an era of colonial exploration and expansion, with Columbus reaching the New World in 1492 and Vasco de Gama discovering a sea route to India in 1497. By the 15th century the science of botany had begun to develop, with the beginnings of plant classification systems and the founding of botanic gardens where exotic specimens could be nurtured and propagated.

Plant hunting became a lucrative business, and the Tradescants (John the Elder and his son, John the Younger) turned it into a career in the

17th century. Historical records are not always clear (and propaganda, hyperbole and obfuscation of information of commercial interest were as rife then as they are now), but the Tradescants are credited with bringing apricots to Britain from Algiers, and the scarlet runner bean from Virginia.

In the 17th century, Sir Joseph Banks joined the Endeavour expedition and brought back more than a thousand new species of plant from Australia and New Zealand, including manuka. He was later responsible for sending plant hunters all over the world, to find more than seven thousand new species (including cash crops). One of those expeditions sent the ill-fated Bounty to collect breadfruit trees from Tahiti, and ended in the infamous mutiny. Captain Bligh survived the experience and eventually completed his task during a second expedition a few years later, the ultimate goal of which was to transplant the breadfruit to the West Indies as a source of food for slaves.

Plant hunting expeditions were a dangerous business, and in the 1800s William Hooker (first director of the Royal Botanic Gardens, Kew) took a more modern approach, relying on his network of overseas contacts to send him new plant samples.

Sir Henry Wickham might have avoided being called a 'bio-pirate' had he followed Hooker's example, but in 1876 he smuggled thousands of rubber tree seeds (*Hevea brasiliensis,* although there are several latex-producing species) back to Kew. From there they were used to found lucrative rubber plantations in Malaya and Singapore.

In 1829 Nathaniel Bagshaw Ward invented the Wardian case - a glazed box like a little greenhouse that allowed plants to thrive in a moist and humid environment during sea voyages, which led to far lower losses. The Wardian case was instrumental in Robert Fortune's clandestine mission in 1848, during which he collected tea plants from China and sent them to India - where they were ultimately used to found new tea plantations in Assam and Sikkim, ending the Chinese monopoly on the tea trade.

The 19th century also saw the establishment of the South American cinchona plant, the source of the quinine that was then the only treatment for malaria, in India and Ceylon. But it wasn't only useful plants that were collected and dispersed - purely ornamental species were also valuable and caused a gardening boom throughout Europe and the colonies.

The advent of air travel and globalisation has made the world, in some senses, a much smaller place. But attitudes towards bio-piracy have hardened, and the life of the modern day plant hunter is very different indeed.

Many of the foods with which we are most familiar were once unusual edibles that aroused suspicion and took a long time to become widely accepted. Take the potato, for example. It has been cultivated in the Andes for 8000 years, but was only 'discovered' in the Old World when it was brought home by Spanish explorers in the 16th century. Initial reactions weren't promising, as the potato is related to poisonous plants such as deadly nightshade, and indeed the foliage (together with any tubers that have been exposed to the sun and turned green) is poisonous.

Sir Walter Raleigh is credited with introducing the potato to the UK and Ireland, although its adoption there is unlikely to have been quite such a simple matter. During the 18th century cultivation of potatoes was actually illegal in France, and the potato only became popular after a determined 'marketing campaign' that included such tricks as guarding 'expensive' potato tubers so badly that the local community pilfered them!

The potato gradually became known as a good food for the poor and hungry, which ironically slowed down its acceptance by everyone else. By the middle of the 19th century it was the staple food of Irish peasants, and when it succumbed to its nemesis – potato blight – it was the trigger (but not the only cause) for the Great Famine, mass starvation and emigration.

Although blight continues to be a problem, fungicides and the development of varieties with some blight resistance have allowed the potato to become a major staple crop in all temperate regions. (Keep an eye out for the blight-resistant Sárpo varieties developed by the Savari Trust.) During WWII the British government created a special character – Potato Pete – to encourage the consumption of potatoes, which were not only a good source of vitamin C but a home-grown staple that supported the UK population through a naval blockade that made importing goods almost impossible.

And in the final years of the 20th century the potato crossed the final frontier, and has been grown in space. It remains a firm favourite with kitchen gardeners on *terra firma,* providing relatively low effort yields and the seasonal delight of serving your own new potatoes. But although *Solanum tuberosum* is familiar, it still holds a few surprises for adventurous gardeners.

In its native South and Central America, the potato comes in thousands of varieties, and several different species. These varieties are cultivated in different places, in different ways, for different purposes. They come in all shapes and sizes and colours, and some have even been bred to be freeze-dried by night frosts for long term storage. These varieties are almost unknown outside of the region, and many would not be suitable for cultivation elsewhere, but some are being used for breeding programs to develop new varieties.

But it is now possible for adventurous gardeners to delve into the potato's past and grow some heritage varieties, propagated in a laboratory into microplants and minitubers that can be grown on to produce tubers with red or blue flesh (some even hold their colour when cooked) or other interesting characteristics.

Interesting varieties are also making a commercial come-back and it is sometimes possible to find tubers sold for eating that you can store and plant in your garden (which is not recommended for novice gardeners as commercial seed potatoes are guaranteed virus-free and are an easy way to ensure that you're not importing plant diseases into your garden).

If you have the space then you could also get involved with breeding your own potato varieties, and there's a lovely blog post by Rebsie (at http://daughterofthesoil.blogspot.co.uk/2010/06/how-to-breed-your-own-potatoes.html) on how to get started. She's also published a book on the subject – The Lost Art of Potato Breeding – through Skylight Press.

If you want to move beyond the potato then there are several other Andean root and tuber crops (some of the 'Lost Crops of the Incas') that may fit the bill – keep an eye out for oca, ulluco, yacón and mashua.

Potatoes and tomatoes have a lot in common. They're both very popular edibles (botanically-speaking the tomato is a fruit, but it is more commonly considered to be a vegetable), they're both from South America and they're both in the same plant family. The cultivated tomato has traditionally been known as *Lycopersicon esculentum,* but taxonomists have now changed the name to *Solanum lycopersicum* to reflect the family relationship.

Just like the potato, this plant that we would be lost without was brought to Europe by Spanish explorers in the early 16th century, from where it spread to Spanish colonies in the Caribbean, the Philippines and on into Asia as well as the rest of Europe.

The English, once again, regarded it with suspicion due to its poisonous relatives. It wasn't grown here until the end of the century – and then only as an ornamental. This wariness spread to England's North American colonies, and it wasn't until the mid-18th century that tomatoes became popular. The Victorians then took to them wholeheartedly and started large-scale cultivation in their new glasshouses.

Tomatoes have now gone full-circle and are renowned for their health-giving properties, including an ability to guard against cancer. They're not completely benign as Kew's researchers have recently discovered that their hairy stems are capable of catching and 'eating' insects (they're one of a number of plants newly discovered to be 'carnivorous'). They are cultivated on all continents (even Antarctica, but only hydroponically, in a special greenhouse). Tomato seeds have a tendency to pass through the human digestion and can occasionally make it through sewage treatment plants to thrive at the clean water outlet – they're pretty tough! And the tomato even plays a starring role in a Spanish festival; La Tomatina takes place near Valencia every August, and culminates in a tomato fight on the streets where everyone gets pelted.

The cultivated tomato still has wild relatives in the deserts of western South America, but adventurous gardeners usually stick to searching out interesting heritage and heirloom varieties – of which there is an incredible variety, in colours right through from white to black. If you want to look further afield then there are plenty of similar fruits that are far more unusual. Try tomatillos for a savoury taste; cape gooseberries or goldenberries, wonderberries, pepinos and tree tomatoes or tamarillos are all sweeter.

When Christopher Columbus went looking for the Indies and found the Americas instead, he brought the New World to the attention of the Old World. He also brought the chilli pepper to Europe, although it had been consumed by the Native Americans for more than 7000 years and domesticated for around 5000. As an alternative spice to the expensive black pepper, the chilli was introduced to South Asia in the 16th century and from there travelled to China and South East Asia. Unlike the potato and the tomato, the pepper seems to have been almost immediately accepted everywhere it went.

And so *Capsicum annuum* has spread throughout the world in its many guises - some large and sweet, some small and spicy. There are many varieties of pepper than can be grown even in a cooler climate. If you want to grow them outside then pick a sunny spot, choose an early variety and hope for a long autumn.

But there are other species of pepper that haven't made it as far from their homeland. *C. frutescens* (the pepper used in Tabasco sauce) and *C. chinense* prefer tropical climates. But the rocoto (also known as the locoto), *C. pubescens,* originates from higher altitudes and prefers cooler weather - it is the most cold-hardy species. A perennial, it can grow quite large and is also known as the tree chilli. Although its fruits come in a range of colours and sizes, they are all hot. And they're not reliably self-fertile like most peppers, so having more than one specimen is recommended.

The ají is the only species apart from *C. annuum* that has spicy and sweet varieties. It is *C. baccatum,* and plants have a tendency to grow very tall. They can also be overwintered with protection, and yields are said to increase as the years go by. The only sweet ají variety I have seen available is from Real Seeds, and it's an ideal choice for those of us who want to add the flavour of a chilli without succumbing to its heat.

C. annuum varieties like lots and lots of light, and it's a fair bet that the related species do as well. They can drop their leaves indoors in the winter when light levels are low; they will resprout in spring but not necessarily early enough to beat newly sown seedlings, so *C. annuum* is usually grown as an annual in the UK. They happily fruit when confined to pots, and are usually self-fertile and so can be grown indoors. Giving plants a gentle shake when they're flowering can help the transfer of pollen; a high potash feed is advisable once they start to flower, to encourage a good crop.

C. annuum peppers are some of my favourite plants - they have handsome dark green and glossy leaves, white star-shaped flowers and then fruits that change from one colour to another. I used to grow them on my desk at work (it turns out they enjoyed the constant fluorescent lighting more than I did) and they were a real conversation starter.

Chilli seeds are widely traded, particularly the really hot ones, as people seem to relish the chance to grow something that makes their head explode. If you're looking to expand your chilli horizons, chilli fiestas have begun to spring up all over the UK and are a great place to find seeds and plants and to try various chilli-enhanced foods.

Runner beans are one of the quintessential vegetable crops for a British kitchen garden. Wherever veg growers gather, you'll hear them discussing their 'runners' – from the perfect point to plant them out (as they are frost tender), to whether the weather conditions are going to be conducive to a 'good set', or whether the flowers are dropping off without being pollinated. The resulting beans are endlessly popular on British dinner tables, too, and it's hard to imagine that this wasn't always the case.

But in fact the runner bean (*Phaseolus coccineus*) is yet another native of Central America, occurring naturally in cool, mountainous regions from Mexico to Panama. It is known to have been in cultivation for over 2000 years, but it didn't arrive in Europe until it was brought there in 1633 by John Tradescant (the elder), who was a plant collector and gardener to Charles 1. His son (also John) succeeded him in these endeavours and together they are credited with introducing numerous familiar plants into Britain. They're both buried at the Museum of Garden History, which is housed in the restored church of St-Mary-at-Lambeth in London.

The runner bean (or scarlet runner) was originally introduced into Britain as an ornamental plant, and wasn't added to kitchen gardens until later, although it certainly appears in vegetable seed catalogues by the 19th century.

You can head back in time and grow heritage varieties of runner bean, which are available with white (as well as the usual scarlet) flowers. Although naturally a climber, modern breeding has produced dwarf varieties (such as Hestia) which are more suited to small gardens.

Outside the UK, French beans (*Phaseolus vulgaris*) tend to be more popular and there are hundreds and hundreds of varieties to try, from modern stringless ones back through the heirloom varieties developed by generations past. They, too, come in both dwarf and climbing forms and with different colour flowers; French beans can also be found with yellow or purple pods.

For something slightly more unusual, but easy to grow, try the Pea bean (*Phaseolus vulgaris* syn. *P. aegypticus);* the Yard Long bean (*Vigna unguiculata* subsp. *sesquipedalis*) is less hardy, and so trickier to grow, but a successful crop would be very impressive for an intrepid gardener. The Lab Lab, or hyacinth bean (*Lablab purpureus),* would likewise be tricky to grow, but its purple pods are gorgeous.

Antarctica

As well as the plant hunters seeking out plants that are new to science and in need of conservation, there are also pioneers attempting to take plants to places they have never been before. We've already seen that the potato has been blasted into space, but plants are also being cultivated in Antarctica - one of the most inhospitable regions on Earth.

With an altitude of around 3000 metres, the Antarctic Plateau is the coldest place on earth. During the Antarctic winter (from mid-February to mid-October), the sun doesn't rise at all. Antarctica experiences a coreless winter - the temperature drops rapidly at the end of the summer, and doesn't rise again until the end of winter. Unlike other places on the planet, there is no one month that is generally the coldest; winter temperatures are approximately constant. Even in summer the average temperature on the Plateau is around −28° Celsius (it's positively balmy on the coast, at −2° Celsius).

And activities in Antarctica are strictly controlled, by the Antarctic Treaty, to preserve the environment. The import of soil and seeds is restricted, except for the seeds of edible plants to be grown in greenhouses.

The original greenhouse at the McMurdo Station, the base for American science operations in Antarctica, has fans to provide air movement and is lit from 7 am to 10 or 11 pm every day. It grows nasturtiums, pansies, spinach, rocket, cucumbers, tomatoes, herbs and chilli peppers, with a special cooler room just for the lettuces.

But the McMurdo greenhouse, still running, was upstaged in 2004 by the 370 square foot South Pole Food Growth Chamber (SPFGC), which adds strawberries, melons and watermelons, kale, sunflowers and other edible flowers to the crop list.

The effect these green spaces have on the local community is immense - they are morale boosters (particularly during the long winters), provide fresh food where canned and frozen goods are on the menu every day, and allows researchers to relax in humid air and bright lighting, helping to alleviate SAD and sleep disorders. They have even been the inspiration for art projects.

Their official purpose is to investigate how human populations could sustain themselves in space and on other planets. The environment has to be completely controlled, with plants grown hydroponically and all of their needs met by human attendants and automated systems. In Antarctica, of course, water is not in short supply. But there are other challenges, including a lack of pollinating insects. Pollination has to be done manually, or encouraged with air currents.

In the future, modules like this could be fully integrated into human systems, removing carbon dioxide from the air and producing oxygen, and recycling waste products. In the meantime, producing anything edible in the Antarctic landscape is an incredible achievement in its own right.

One Giant Leap

Antarctica isn't the only inhospitable landscape on the planet for humans; we find it hard to live underwater as well. But the idea of living under the sea is a romantic one, and features fairly often in science fiction. If we don't get global warming under control, and sea levels rise dramatically, then it's a lifestyle our descendants may be obliged to adopt in the future. Of course, the oceans are home to plants and animals, and we already rely on them for a portion of our food supply. But if we wanted to carry on eating the same things underwater then we'd need artificially-lit, controlled environments very similar to those we would need in space.

NASA makes use of an underwater laboratory off the Florida Keys for astronaut training (although here they're called aquanauts). It allows them to carry out necessary tasks in a similarly hostile environment to space - although the decompression process means it takes longer to return to the surface!

It doesn't look like much experimentation has been done in the way of growing terrestrial plants underwater, but in 2007 botanist Lloyd Godson spent some time in his BioSub, submerged in a flooded gravel pit for nearly two weeks. His food was provided from the surface, but he did use the alga *Chlorella* to remove carbon dioxide from the atmosphere and produce oxygen; shortly before the end of the stay there was enough for him to nibble on, as *Chlorella* is also edible.

The space plants take up, and their weight, would be less of an issue underwater than they would be during a space mission, but a space journey of any length (such as a manned mission to Mars) would be more feasible if the astronauts could grow some of their own food, and use plants to produce oxygen and purify water. These plants would need to be multi-tasking, easily grown and small, and to have few inedible parts. The list of potential space crops so far includes lettuce, spinach, carrots, tomatoes, green onions, radishes, bell peppers, strawberries, fresh herbs and cabbages.

It's a big job description for a small plant, but there have already been plenty of experiments to find out whether they can even survive in space. In a long partnership with Park Seed, NASA's SEEDS in Space project sent many different species into orbit. Once the seeds were back on Earth, they were distributed to schools for experiments to see how they had been affected by their trip - not much, it seems. Space is a nice environment for many seeds - it's cold and dry. But long-term exposure to the vacuum of space would deprive seeds of the small amounts of oxygen they need to stay alive.

That was all in the late 20th century, but since then there has been a real 'garden' in space, with astronauts experimenting with germinating and growing plants, harvesting the crop and bringing it back to Earth for appraisal. There are concerns about whether the growth of harmful microorganisms will be a problem in space, and whether the unusual conditions (including minimal irrigation) would cause the plants to take up too many salts. Mizuna, lettuce, peas and radishes have all had extraterrestrial experiences.

It looks as though it will be the plants doing most of the exploring from now on!

CHAPTER TWO

Modern day plant hunters

Throughout the 20th century humanity became increasingly aware of the damage it was doing to the environment, and in 1948 the IUCN (International Union for Conservation of Nature) was formed. It produced its first list of threatened plants in 1970, naming 20,000 species. Even though new lists have been produced since then, they still probably only cite a small fraction of the plant species that are actually in trouble. And scientists estimate that up to 25% of plant species remain unknown to science.

In 1975 CITES (the Convention on International Trade in Endangered Species) came into force. It holds three lists of plant species, all controlled to different extents. The idea behind CITES is to prevent international trade causing the over-exploitation of the named species; 30,000 plants are covered.

Since then there has been a marked change to conservation strategies, as it has become clear that protecting individual species is not enough - we need to conserve entire habitats if the species they contain have a hope of survival. Thirty-four regions have been termed biodiversity hot spots. Although they cover a mere two or three percent of Earth's surface, over half the world's plant species are endemic to these regions. Sadly more than 80% of hot spot habitats have already been damaged, and so it is here that conservation efforts are focused.

The role of botanic gardens has changed considerably since we started to create them. Initially they were physic gardens, designed to contain medicinal plant species and to educate medical practitioners. During the colonial period they became triumphant showcases of exotic species, but the modern botanic garden's aims are conservation and education.

In 2005 a new botanic garden, the Royal Botanic Garden of Jordan, was founded in Amman. Its aim is to preserve native plants, an important endeavour as the wild relatives of crop species including wheat, oats, barley, garlic and onions, lentils and apricots are found in the region. And the Svalbard Global Seed Bank, in arctic Norway, holds reserves of the seeds of crop plants, as an insurance policy against disaster and also as a gene bank conserving genetic diversity that could be bred back into future crop varieties.

The Millennium Seed Bank (MSB) is housed at Kew's second garden (Wakehurst Place) in West Sussex, safely away from the river Thames at the main Kew garden that could cause problems with flooding. Its aim is to collect seeds from every wild plant species on the planet (many of these species are edible or otherwise useful, even though they are not in cultivation). Seeds are collected, identified and processed throughout the world, and sent for cold storage at the MSB. (Orthodox seeds can be safely stored for years if they are properly dried and kept suitably cool; a far smaller number of recalcitrant species do not respond to this treatment and have to be conserved as living plants.)

Seed banks are very useful repositories for seeds, which are regularly removed from storage and grown into mature plants from which a fresh batch of seeds can be collected and stored. Seeds are also taken out of the seed banks and used for new crop development, or the reestablishment of damaged habitats.

Seed banks are also a hot bed of scientific experimentation, developing new techniques for germinating seeds, or propagating problem plants. These techniques can be used to revive ancient seed samples. Seeds were often buried with mummies in Peru, and the dry climate there means the seeds can remain in a viable state. And in 2006 scientists from the MSB managed to germinate seeds that had been stuck in a notebook by a Dutch merchant in 1803 - they revived three species, a legume, an acacia and a protea, despite the poor conditions in which the seeds had been stored.

In 2012 it was announced that a team of Russian scientists had produced live plants of the narrow-leafed campion, from seeds that had been buried for 32,000 years. Although the fruits discovered in the burrow of an arctic ground squirrel were unable to germinate, the team managed to use micropropagation techniques to clone new plants from cells in the seeds that were still alive. Their results have yet to be confirmed, so it is too soon to say that an extinct plant has been resurrected, but the plants grown flowered and set seed, and those seeds have normal germination rates.

The MSB works with partner organisations in many countries, spreading their expertise on collecting and preserving seeds and plants as well as collecting information about their uses and distribution. With concerns about bio-piracy on the political agenda, not all of these seeds (and their corresponding information) is being brought back to the UK - some remains in the country of origin and is used to foster local conservation efforts.

Although most plant hunting these days is done by scientists, there are a few commercial hunters remaining, finding new plants and bringing them into cultivation. Bleddyn and Sue Wynn-Jones from Crûg Farm Plants have been on numerous plant hunting trips, bringing back mainly ornamental species to their nursery in North Wales. And botanical tours of India, Nepal, Sikkim and Japan have added to the edible and medicinal herb species on offer from Poyntzfield Herb Nursery in Scotland. Paul Barney of Edulis has made plant-hunting trips to add to his stock of unusual plants, and Joy Larkcom was instrumental in bringing salad plants and oriental vegetables to the UK and beyond. There are many more amateur plant hunters who are seeking out unusual edibles to grow on their plots.

Joan Lambert Bailey

Joan Lambert Bailey divides her time between working on an organic farm in Tokyo, and writing about the small farms and gardens that dot the landscape. After moving to Tokyo from rural Michigan in 2009, Joan exchanged chickens, coyotes, and flocks of wild turkeys for urban organic farming and learning all she can about the myriad farms and gardens that seem to fill every spare nook and cranny of this booming metropolis. She shares her observations and adventures growing, harvesting, and preserving all of these fantastic new foods at www.japanfarmersmarkets.com.

What unusual edibles do you grow?

I realize now that this might be a bit tricky. Almost anything I grow in my Tokyo garden that satisfies my American palate is an unusual edible. This summer I grew Black Dakota popcorn, three kinds of kale, bergamot, yacón, beets, Swiss chard and rhubarb as some of my crops.

I've been growing popcorn in my garden for more than seven years. I began with Japanese hulless, but found it unsatisfying in terms of taste and cob size. I experimented then with a larger yellow variety, and gradually began mixing varieties. Our final year in Michigan I grew three – Tom Thumb, a small yellow kernel; Strawberry with lovely mid-size cobs and red kernels; and Thanksgiving, a large cob with brown kernels – and much to my delight I ended up with a number of colorful cross-pollinated cobs. Thanksgiving is easily my favorite – an heirloom I purchased from Project Grow Community Gardens – for its flavor, color, and terrific growth. I'm hopeful this year's Dakota Black turns out as well.

Kale is grown in Japan only as an ornamental for the winter months. Growing three different kinds – Laciento, Red Russian, and Blue Curly – may seem over the top, but we dearly miss those giant leaves in salads, soups, and sandwiches. The farmers I work with are still a bit unsure about my seeming obsession with the plant, and dutifully munch on it when I bring a dish round to share. I figure since they fell in love with pesto on the first spoonful, they may eventually gain affection for my favorite leafy green.

Bergamot (bee balm or monarda) is a native plant in Michigan, and I fell for it first because of its lovely blossom. A woodland flower, it is also a favorite of an assortment of pollinators, and I decided to include it in my perennial bed. Unbeknownst to me bergamot also happens to be a key ingredient in a handful of wonderfully tasty Lebanese dishes. Once our Lebanese neighbor discovered it our tables filled with a most-fantastic potato salad that we fought over at potlucks. Rare in Japan, a friend shared a seedling and when I spotted some at a local nursery I bought the lot. I still grow it for the flowers and to attract beneficials, but we also savor the taste of home, too.

[The potato salad recipe is available from Joan's blog, at http://www.japanfarmersmarkets.com/2010/05/bergamont-in-pot.html. *She says that it seems to be best made in small batches, and served warm.]*

Yacón, a South American potato-like thing, is a somewhat new vegetable in Japan. A woman I met at a fall harvest gathering last year sent me a box full of seedlings earlier this spring, and the yacón were among them. A root vegetable with the texture of an apple and the sweetness of a pear, yacón is quite lovely raw in salad and cooked up in a stir-fry. I'm hoping to do a bit of seed-saving when the time comes, but we'll see. The intensely hot summer and subsequent drought have rendered them short and not as happy as I might like to see them. Regardless, I'm looking forward to and hopeful for the harvest.

Japanese winter vegetables have proven to be one of my most pleasant surprises. Daikon, kabu, shungiku (chrysanthemum greens), and komatsuna are welcome additions to our home table. Of these, perhaps the strangest for Western tastebuds might be shungiku. Late last fall as I put the seeds in the ground in a cold rain I remember thinking "Why am I doing this? What the hell are edible chrysanthemum greens, anyway?" But I obviously carried on as the farmers had shared their seeds with

21

me, and thought they seemed a logical choice. Now they, too, are a favorite dish for our table (my mouth is watering even as I type this) served warm or cold with soy sauce, sugar, and sesame seeds.

On our balcony garden I grew goya (Okinawan bitter melon) as a green curtain this summer. Strong vines with large leaves wound their way up, and the long warty fruit also graced our table with its funky flavor. Undoubtedly bitter, goya earns its name with every morsel, but somehow keeps us coming back for more. I still don't have a great recipe, so we mostly eat it in salads for the time being.

How did your interest in unusual edibles develop?

We grew popcorn when I was a child one year. I remember shucking the cobs with my mother in the kitchen, and thinking how cool it was to have grown our own. I'm not sure what inspired her exactly, but I think it may have been a time when electric poppers emerged on the market. My parents weren't exactly trend setters, but there must have been some appeal there. A good friend in college was mad about popcorn, and I've not looked back since. Some advice I got while trying to decide what to grow in my first garden was grow what you like to eat. Despite a naysayer or two, I planted my own first seeds in my second (and substantially larger) garden. There's nothing better than munching on popcorn from your own garden.

The best way to get to know a foreign culture, whether living there or visiting, is through food. A good meal or a chat about growing a certain vegetable, herb or fruit is an easy way to bridge gaps and get to know people. Japan has been no exception, and is certainly home to a number of new fruits and vegetables that I've never seen or tasted before. I'm looking forward to trying my hand next season at satoimo (literally translated as "country potato"), which has a beautiful, beautiful leaf and good flavor if not overcooked. Overcooking brings out the slimy side of the vegetable, which I cannot say is my preference.

How do you track down your unusual seeds and plants?

It depends on what's available when I stop by any of the assorted nurseries. Often it's pure chance that I spot a plant or a seed packet. And somehow some vegetable seeds meander their way over from America, too.

Do you have a favourite supplier?

Seed Saver Exchange and Seeds of Change are where I find the best selection of interesting popcorn varieties, although now many organizations organize seed swaps that offer a bevy of funky stuff. Otherwise it's friends or luck of the draw.

Do you have books and/or websites that you recommend?

The Earth Knows My Name: Food, Culture, and Sustainability in the Gardens of Ethnic Americans by Patricia Klindienst, 2006. Beacon Press. An amazingly well-written book about food and culture being a touchstone for identity. I love this book, and I wrote a review of it a while back.

Do you have a favourite garden to visit that grows a lot of unusual edibles?

Hmmm... not one that springs to mind....

What are your hints and tips for sourcing unusual edibles?

I say head to a foreign country and see what's cooking and growing. Or head to a local farmer's market or area of town dominated by an immigrant community. Walk around grocery stores or peek over garden walls, and then strike up a conversation. My bet is that a seedling with growing instructions and a recipe will head home with you in no time.

Stephen Barstow

Stephen Barstow is an Englishman living in Norway, with the most incredible collection of edible plants - despite a cold climate in which the sun does not come up at all in the winter. He coined the term 'edimentals' to describe ornamental edible plants, and spent three days putting together the world's largest salad - it contained 536 ingredients. And that's a small fraction of the edible plants in the world, thought to be around 15,000.

Stephen has written several interesting articles for Permaculture Magazine, and you can download PDF copies from my website (http://emmacooper.org/blog/forthcoming-book-around-the-world-in-80-plants). Xtreme Salads tells the story of Stephen's record-breaking salads. Caucasian Spinach is all about *Hablitzia tamnoides* and Oriental Perennial Spinach introduces you to the delights of edible hostas. You can find out more about *Hablitzia* in Stephen's Facebook group (http://www.facebook.com/groups/hablitzia).

Stephen's first book, "Around the world in 80 plants: an edible perennial vegetable adventure in temperate climates", was published by Permanent Publications in November 2014.

What unusual edibles do you grow?

To answer this would need a book (or several), but I've planted several thousand different edibles in my garden. I'm most interested in perennials, and hardy plants in particular - plants that can survive a several month winter freeze with little or no light (I am close to the Arctic Circle) and minimum temperatures down to -25°C. They also need to stand low summer temperatures (in some summers we may only get a few days above 20°C, but it varies tremendously from year to year!). There are many species to choose from – remember that the UK has a very mild climate for its latitude! Consequently, I'm interested in plants from most of the temperate world, in particular plants originating from northern Europe, the mountains of southern Europe, the Caucasus, Russia, the Himalayas, northern China, Siberia, Japan, Korea and North

America. As coordinator of the Norwegian Seed Savers (Planteklubben for Grønnsaker) I also grow a good range of Norwegian heirloom vegetables (seed propagated and perennials).

How did your interest in unusual edibles develop?

I moved to Norway in the early 1980s at a time when there were very few vegetables available in shops and people I met were often of the opinion that the reason for only potatoes, carrots and cabbage being available was simply that it was difficult to grow much more than that. This was far from the truth and I guess I subconsciously set out to prove them wrong – possibly the most diverse vegetable garden in Europe located close to the Arctic Circle sounds a bit unlikely.... I was also inspired by the local group of the over 100-year old Nyttevekstforeningen (literally, Useful Plants Society). This society is as far as I know unique - I know of no other country with a society dedicated to its wild useful plants. During local spring foraging forays I would learn a whole range of local wild plants which were excellent wild greens – nettles, caraway, ostrich fern, giant bellflower and field garlic to name just a few, and a host of seaweed species added variety to the menu. Our leader, Jan Erik Kofoed, would often demonstrate underwater foraging, though his pupils were reluctant to follow suit (temperature in the fjord was perhaps only 10°C at this time of year)! Many of the 60 or so wild edibles I could find within a mile or so of my house were perennials. In autumn fungi, very popular here, were the subject of the group's foraging activities. When my kids arrived, I had less time for foraging and I planted some of my favourite local species in the garden for ease of access. Then, on a work trip to the US around 1990, I stumbled upon a herb magazine, Herb Companion, and in it was an advert for the Abundant Seed Foundation (set up to supply seed to the needy in 3rd world countries). I sent off for their seed catalogue and in that I saw an interesting sounding book for sale – Sturtevant's Edible Plants of the World. Compiled by Professor Sturtevant in the latter part of the 19th and early 20th century, it is basically an extensive list (some 3,000 species) of edible plants (many wild sourced) with short notes on use with comprehensive references. A quick estimate reveals that some 90% of these as perennials. I don't remember how I first heard of Ken Fern and Plants for a Future (probably through the HDRA?), but when he kindly sent me the complete PFAF database on a set of diskettes some time in the early 1990s, I was completely hooked on unusual edibles. I must have accessed Ken's database tens of thousands of times in the intervening years, mainly on the net!

How do you track down your unusual seeds and plants?

Internet trading has been my main method of quickly accumulating a large collection of edibles for trialling. Each year over the last 15 years I've saved seed from my own plants and made a seed list which I've posted on various trading sites on the Internet (before that there were off-line trading clubs) together with my own wish list. With a bit of effort one can get hold of most things this way for little more than postage. In recent years I've also been a member of various "rock garden" clubs who publish extensive lists of seed each year, by no means only alpines (it's the eyes that see...)! – I remember reading an article in Herb Companion by a leading herbalist who said that one of his best sources of unusual herbs was the North American Rock Garden Club's (NARGS) seed list. He was right.... Seed Savers Exchange in the US is also an excellent source (some 13,500 unique varieties in 2010) – although mostly traditional vegetables, there are a number of unusual edibles listed, particularly in the "Miscellaneous" section. I've also sourced more unusual things from some specialist seed sellers such as Berkutenko's seed list of wild collected seed from Magadan and the Russian Far East. For plants, the on-line RHS Plant Finder is very useful and this led me originally to Paul Barney's Edulis, a nursery specializing in unusual edibles and permaculture plants. Another of course is Martin Crawford who has possibly the best commercial seed list dedicated to unusual edibles. However, I mustn't forget all those generous local gardeners who have given me cuttings and plants over the years! Another useful source is through taking part on relevant Internet discussion forums. My favourites are Homegrown Goodness, http://alanbishop.proboards.com (here you will find many experienced and experimental growers, many breeding their own vegetables, inspired by Carol Deppe's book Breeding Your Own Vegetables) and the Scottish Rock Garden Club Forum (http://www.srgc.net/forum/index.php).

Do you have a favourite (commercial) supplier?

Martin Crawford (ART) and Edulis.

Do you have books and/or websites that you recommend?

The most useful reference book on unusual edibles is undoubtedly Stephen Facciola's Cornucopia II, but you have to pay an arm and a leg to get hold of a copy these days (time for a new edition). It covers 3,000 species (unlike PFAF, both temperate and tropical) with a short description of the edible use with references. There's very little information on Facciola out there – love to know more about him. For interesting/potential North American species and inspiration, I would recommend Samuel Thayer's two foraging books. Simply the best foraging books I've read – thorough and it reflects Sam's personal hands-on experience. I should of course also mention Ken Fern's book! Joy Larkcom's Oriental Vegetables is a good start for the Far East, including a few of the many wild species used in that region.

Do you have a favourite garden to visit that grows a lot of unusual edibles?

For me, I would have to say Kew Gardens (Oxford, Cambridge and Edinburgh botanics are also personal favourites that I visit when I get the chance) and other botanical gardens around the world. However, none of them have dedicated ethnobotanical gardens. My favourite would be a small botanical garden in Firenze (Florence) Italy which I literally stumbled upon one year. It has a section dedicated to wild foraged Tuscany edibles, some 150+ species, with short culinary information on the plant labels. Many of them will also be familiar to Northern Europeans. Otherwise, my friend Frank van Kiersbilck in

Belgium has a great collection of edibles – his main interest is in Andean/South American edibles (I call his garden "Andes in Flanders"). Many of the Andean tubers such as Ulluco, Oca, Yacón... and even potato are essentially perennials which we harvest for the winter and replant in the spring. Martin Crawford's forest garden and trials area is the most interesting I've seen for unusual edible trees and bushes.

Charlotte Benditt

Charlotte Benditt is originally from Pennsylvania (USA), but currently resides in Oxfordshire (UK). You can follow her gardening exploits on Twitter (@sbeneli).

What unusual edibles do you grow?

2010 was my first year with an allotment, which has spread over to container gardening in my back garden. I sowed so many back-up seedlings that I then couldn't bear to part with! In addition to "usual" edibles, I'm growing achocha, West Indian gherkins, rat's tail radishes, celtuce, asparagus peas, and sweet pea currant tomatoes. There are some things I'm growing that I consider to be quite usual but which others seem to think are a bit off the beaten path, such as mooli, choi sum, gai lan, tomatillos, and mibuna.

How did your interest in unusual edibles develop?

For me, the opportunity to grow my own food meant also the opportunity to grow things which I can't find in the supermarket or for which I have to make a special trip to an ethnic grocery in order to purchase. I've always been an adventurous cook and have always sought out new things to try.

How do you track down your unusual seeds and plants?

I've found that a lot of independent companies that specialize in heirloom seeds tend to have all sorts of exciting varieties to try. My wish list for the next growing season has about 40 different things, and most of them have been found by first finding a supplier and seeing what they offer. Online swaps are also really useful for finding new seeds to try.

Do you have a favourite (commercial) supplier?

I've gotten the most interesting seeds and best customer service from The Real Seed Catalogue.

Do you have books and/or websites that you recommend?

My main source is Grow Your Own Vegetables by Joy Larkcom. Everybody online suggests it, and they really do know what they're talking about! I'm also lucky that my partner's father has had an allotment for 25 years, and while he tends to grow the usual veg, it's been incredibly helpful to have someone experienced who is willing to answer even my silliest questions. Myfolia.com is also a huge help.

Do you have a favourite garden to visit that grows a lot of unusual edibles?

No.

What are your hints and tips for sourcing unusual edibles?

Look at heritage seed companies and engage in seed swaps (either online or events like Seedy Sunday). Mr. Fothergill's Vegetable Explorer range also has some interesting things to try.

Sally Cunningham

Sally Cunningham has been a professional organic gardener for around thirty years. When she moved to Leicester in the early 1980s she became fascinated with the multicultural society there, particularly the unfamiliar food plants she found in Asian supermarkets and markets. Since then she has been collecting these plants, trying to grow them here in the UK, and talking to people about how they are grown and used in the cultures that brought them here.

Sally worked on the Plant Cultures project that looked at the ethnobotany (the uses to which plants are put) of Asian plants – a lovely project website detailed the history and uses of a number of important plants, many of which cannot be grown without help in a temperate climate. In 2009 Sally wrote 'Asian Vegetables', a book that details over 40 edible plants from the Indian subcontinent, together with information on their uses and how to go about growing them yourself, with a list of suppliers.

Sally also played an important role in the Sowing New Seeds project (http://www.sowingnewseeds.org.uk) (based at the Garden Organic HQ, Ryton Gardens), which aims to collect and share resources (both seeds and information) about the unusual edible plants grown this country. Her personal website is http://www.askaboutplants.com.

What unusual edibles do you grow?

Almost everything – you name it, I've grown it – except a few such as mangosteen, pineapple or pawpaw which need extra heat/space. This year I'm growing yard long beans, lemongrass, cinnamon vine, sweet potatoes, green aubergines, amaranth, purslane, tulsi, Chilean myrtle and purple chillies at home.

How and why did your interest in unusual edibles develop?

I've always been interested in edible plants, ever since about the age of four when I helped mum pick bilberries, crab apples and rowan berries.

We foraged because it was there and we were broke, and later on, aged about eight or nine there was the fun of finding out things - like that judas tree flowers were nice too.

How do you track down your unusual seeds and plants?

Ask as many people as I can about what they eat and grow and similar questions; read as much and as widely as possible.

Do you have a favourite supplier?

Probably Chiltern Seeds, Jungle Seeds, tropicalfruitandveg.co.uk, Suffolk Herbs, and don't forget B & T World seeds.

Do you have books and/or websites that you recommend?

Plants for a Future by Ken Fern, Flora Britannica by Richard Mabey, the Purdue University website, Oriental Vegetables by Joy Larkcom.

Do you have a favourite garden to visit that grows a lot of unusual edibles?

It has to be Ryton Organic Garden near Coventry!

What are your hints and tips for sourcing unusual edibles?

Never go past an ethnic supermarket without going in and looking not just at the fresh produce but the dried stuff too. And if you visit a garden make a point of finding a gardener to beg/swop seeds/cuttings from. I carried seeds from the Isle of Man in a driving licence and berries from Scotland tied in a hanky and slept on for two nights but they germinated...!

Sally's publications

Sally's book "Asian Vegetables: A Guide to Growing Fruit, Vegetables and Spices from the Indian Subcontinent" was published by Eco-Logic Books in January 2009.

And Sally has written a book with her Garden Organic colleague, Dr. Anton Rosenfield, called "Sowing New Seeds: A guide to growing unusual crops in the UK". Published by Garden Organic, it's currently only available if you send them a cheque for £5 and ask very nicely!

Alys Fowler

Alys Fowler trained at the Royal Horticultural Society, the New York Botanical Gardens and the Royal Botanic Gardens at Kew. She joined the BBC Gardeners' World team as a researcher, then later took a role in front of the cameras. This led to her presenting her own series - The Edible Garden - in which we watched as she turned her urban back garden into a beautiful, edible paradise.

You can find Alys on Twitter (@alysfowler), and she writes a regular column for the Guardian.

What unusual edibles do you grow?

Mainly pretty perennials, lots of edible flowers, alliums (Victory allium (*Allium victorialis), A. moly,* round-headed leeks), sedums for salads, aquilegia (spring greens, edible flowers). Not cutting edge, but like I say pretty.

How and why did your interest in unusual edibles develop?

I've spent the last five or so years trying to find edibles that fit into very small, mainly urban gardens. I want to find edibles that look good, so that there's none of those 'I don't have space for edibles and I want my garden to look pretty' excuses.

How do you track down your unusual seeds and plants?

Mainly through other individuals either swapping or buying online. Most of my stuff isn't rare, just a little left of fields. A lot come from garden centres where they are grown as ornamentals.

Do you have a favourite supplier?

Avon bulbs for edible bulbs (not that they think of themselves as suppliers of such things). I buy a lot of stuff from Real Seeds, Thomas Etty Seeds, Franchi and Jungle seeds (but all more traditional veg stuff) and the HSL.

Do you have books and/or websites that you recommend?

I find social networks the best place as most of the more interesting stuff has yet to be put in a book. Owen Smith for instance has been a wealth of knowledge on Twitter. Stephen Barstow on Facebook (which is how I first got in touch with him originally), Permaculture Magazine and website. Various American sites and the lovely Martin Crawford's work, endless inspiration there. Most of this lot have much bigger gardens than me, so it's a case of filtering and refining for a small garden.

Do you have a favourite garden to visit that grows a lot of unusual edibles?

Stephen Barstow's garden in Norway still stands out for just being so fascinating and against such a backdrop. We spent three solid days on our hands and knees talking plants. There aren't many places where you can do that on as 45% slope! Stephen's got a book coming out soon. There's so much in that man's head I am very excited to see how it comes out.

What are your hints and tips for sourcing unusual edibles?

Read, search, Google, hunt and nibble carefully. Actually keep tasting at different points in the season and experiment with recipes. It's taken a while for certain plants to work for me culinary wise. I used to think, 'pah that just doesn't taste nice'; now I'm more inclined to say, 'hmm not the right method of cooking. Let's try again.'

Alys' books

Alys sneaks little tidbits about all kinds of unusual edibles into all of her books:

'The Edible Garden: How to Have Your Garden and Eat It', about suburban self-sufficiency, was published by BBC Books in March 2010. Trying to have it all - a beautiful, productive small garden - means lots of lovely edimentals.

'The Thrifty Forager: Living Off Your Local Landscape' is all about looking for edibles that are wild or that have been planted by other people - but that doesn't mean you couldn't give some of them a home in your garden! It was published by Kyle Books in September 2011, and contains a write-up of Alys' visit to Stephen Barstow's garden in Norway.

'The Thrifty Gardener: How to Create a Stylish Garden for Next to Nothing' was published by Kyle Cathie in September 2008.

And, 'Abundance: How to Store and Preserve Your Garden Produce' (which has nothing to do with unusual edibles, but lots of weird preserving) was published in May 2013 by Kyle Books.

Profile: Martin Crawford

Martin Crawford has been running the Agroforestry Forestry Research Trust since 1992. The Trust is a registered charity that researches temperate agroforestry; agroforestry is an umbrella term that describes the use of trees in agriculture, but Martin is particularly famous for his forest garden in Devon (south-west England).

What does Martin grow?

The forest contains upwards of 140 species of trees and shrubs - each chosen because it is edible or otherwise useful. Apples, pears and plums will be familiar to everyone, but visitors may struggle to identify cornelian cherries, Japanese pepper trees and persimmons. Martin is a big supporter of the development of nut crops here in the UK; bladdernuts and hazels are best for smaller gardens. Sweet chestnuts, walnuts, hickories and heartnuts eventually become large trees.

How did Martin's interest in unusual edibles develop?

Over the last 25 years, Martin has taught small-scale organic agriculture, grown food for a small hotel, restored a walled garden and run his own organic market garden and tree nursery. His experiences and an interest in sustainable food production led him towards the forest garden idea.

Hints and tips

To be productive, a forest garden needs to be well thought out and properly planned. Start with a shelter belt, if necessary, to protect the less hardy plants from prevailing winds. And think diversity - Martin's forest garden now contains over 500 different species.

Martin's publications

Martin has several publications about single species, or small groups of plants, that are most easily sourced via his website. His main publications are as follows:

'Creating a Forest Garden: Working with Nature to Grow Edible Crops' is an up-to-date guide on how to plant your own forest garden, complete with plant profiles and colour photographs. It was published by Green Books in April 2010. Ebook versions are also now available.

'A Forest Garden Year' is a DVD that makes a nice companion to the book, although it was published first, in May 2009 (again, by Green Books).

Green Books published 'How to Grow Perennial Vegetables: Low-maintenance, low-impact vegetable gardening' in April 2012.

And Martin wrote 'Food from Your Forest Garden: How to Harvest, Cook and Preserve Your Forest Garden Produce' with Caroline Aitken in May 2013.

Websites

At the ART website you can buy seeds and plants and Martin's other publications (including the quarterly Agrofrestry News). You can also find details of his courses and open days.

http://www.agroforestry.co.uk

Mike Hannon

Mike Hannon and his wife have chosen a path towards all aspects of self-reliance in their lives, which he chronicles on his blog Subsistence Pattern (http://subsistencepatternfoodgarden.blogspot.com). Their main focus is on growing and gathering their own food, in North Idaho in the USA.

What unusual edibles do you grow?

For the most part we grow an ever-increasing number of interesting plants that are not common in the average garden in our area, including: Strawberry Spinach (beetberry), epazote, soapwort, scorzonera & salsify, sea kale, ground cherry & Giant Cape Gooseberry, litchi tomato (Morelle de Balbis), honeyberry, sunchokes, josta berries, perilla (shiso), spilanthes, walking onions, Mexican gherkins, many different varieties of potatoes & tomatoes, and new to us this year Devil's Apple - a member of the eggplant family that contains an active ingredient which is being studied as a possible skin cancer treatment.

How and why did your interest in unusual edibles develop?

My interest in unusual edibles revolves around my fascination with gardening and the consumption of foods in their most natural state. First and foremost our garden is set up to provide a year-round supply of nutritious foods that help us to achieve the self-sufficient lifestyle that we enjoy. That said, over the years I have come to realize that there are many more plants available that are not normally grown in my climate and that can and do thrive in our gardens providing us with a valuable source of nutrient-dense food.

The first "unusual" edible that I ever grew was a tomatillo plant, now a staple in our diet. Each and every year we try to incorporate something new into the gardens and are always amazed that many of the plants follow the same path as the tomatillo, becoming an important part of our diet and lifestyle.

How do you track down your unusual seeds and plants?

I track down seeds and plants by reading blogs, internet articles, browsing seed catalogues, and through the reading of old gardening books. I am especially interested in Victorian kitchen gardens of the past and have adopted many of their methods into my own gardens.

Do you have a favourite supplier?

We do not have any one favorite supplier preferring to use any and all sources available. Honestly, over the years our biggest supplier of seeds has become our own garden as we have spent much time and effort in becoming more self-reliant by learning how to save our own seeds.

Do you have books and/or websites that you recommend?

I have greatly enjoyed reading 'The Victorian Kitchen Garden' by Jennifer Davis and watching video clips from the BBC television series of the same name starring the late Harry Dodson. Books such as 'The Kitchen Gardens at Heligan' by Tom Petherick & Melanie Eclare are also valuable resources, full of information regarding vegetables of old. I was first introduced to the art of forcing vegetables such as Belgian endive and other great crops like scorzonera and salsify via these great sources of information.

[*Mike's forcing efforts are now legendary – check out his blog post http://subsistencepatternfoodgarden.blogspot.co.uk/2010/01/basement-full-of-garden.html.*]

What are your hints and tips for sourcing unusual edibles?

I find that one of the best ways to source unusual edibles is to scour the numerous heirloom seed catalogues such as Baker Creek Heirloom Seeds as many of these gardening catalogue companies are always on the hunt for new and exciting additions to their yearly listings. Following others blogs has also been a very fine source of information regarding different varieties of plants and how they are grown.

Maddy Harland

Maddy and Tim Harland established Permanent Publications in 1990 and since then have published books on a wide range of sustainability issues, including important books on unusual edibles and sustainable gardening such as Plants for a Future by Ken Fern and How to Make a Forest Garden by Patrick Whitefield. All of their books (and more) are available from their Green Shopping Catalogue.

They brought Permaculture Magazine into the world in 1992, and it regularly features unusual edible and useful plants, the people who grow them and general techniques for earth-friendly gardening.

Whilst they were bringing their business to life, and raising a family, they were also creating a permaculture paradise of their own in their back garden. They have a beautiful forest garden that is teeming with wildlife, and a productive permaculture veg plot as well, and they're big fans of unusual edibles.

What unusual edibles do you grow?

Mainly things like Siberian Pea Tree, Goji berries, Chinese quince and dogwood, Yellowhorn (a strange Chinese nut tree), Nepalese Pepper tree, heirloom vegetables, medlar, poke weed (edible when cooked), perennial kale....

After a visit to the Agroforestry Research Trust we added the following trees to our forest garden in 2010: Persimmon (*Diospyros kaki)* Mazelli, Chinese quince (*Pseudocydonia sinensis),* Yellowhorn (*Xanthoceras sorbifolium).* New groundcover plants include the Nepalese raspberry (*Rubus nepalensis)* and Emerald Carpet (*Rubus pentalobus).*

How and why did your interest in unusual edibles develop?

Because I planted normal fruit and nut trees and wanted something different to try out and then I am lazy and want to eat perennials!

How do you track down your unusual seeds and plants?

Agroforestry research trust (ART), Emma Cooper, cuttings from mates, some seed catalogues.

Do you have books and/or websites that you recommend?

Perennial Vegetables by Eric Toensmeier, Permaculture Magazine, Stephen Barlow's book on perennial crops. Emma Cooper's Alternative Kitchen Garden blog (http://emmacooper.org/blog) and podcast (http://emmacooper.org/podcast).

Do you have a favourite garden to visit that grows a lot of unusual edibles?

ART, and mine!

What are your hints and tips for sourcing unusual edibles?

Make sure they taste nice – not all the ones that are meant to are actually edible – they may not poison you but things like Good King Henry are awful.

Søren Holt

Søren Holt is a keen seed saver and plant breeder and blogs about his small garden in Denmark at In the Toad's Garden (http://toads.wordpress.com).

What unusual edibles do you grow?

I believe in the power of diversity. What I can do for diversity is to grow it. If I have access to useful varieties, I grow them. This is true for peas, beans, squash, tomatoes, turnips, kale etc. With these I grow different varieties, to find my favourites. And when I do have favourites, I still try new varieties out of curiosity.

But there are crops that are not suited to my northern climate in Denmark. Melons, eggplants and peppers are not considered possible to grow out in the ground. These I work on, in the hope to breed suitable varieties. There's no chance any professional breeder would do the job. I could wait for another amateur gardener to do it, or give it a try myself.

I also grow some old-time and forgotten vegetables, like Hablitzia and mercury, or exotic stuff like yacón, oca, lemongrass. I even go to the extreme, to grow things I don't believe can survive in my greenhouse. These usually fail with excellence, like the black pepper cuttings send to me from a gardener in Malaysia. But sometimes I find a way to culture some of these, like my greater galangal, that thrives in my greenhouse in the shadow under the tomatoes during the summer season, and in a spot out of direct sunshine inside my house during the three cold seasons.

How did your interest in unusual edibles develop?

I'm the kind of person who gets interested when I gain access to the unusual edibles. I'm curious, want to grow it, to find out if it's easy enough to grow, and taste, if it's worth growing for the space it takes in the garden.

How do you track down your unusual seeds and plants?

I'm a member of the Danish seed savers. We share an extensive exchange list. I also swap seeds on the internet. As soon as you have something unusual to offer, you will get some unusual offers also. I also understand German, and there are a lot of very serious seed savers in German-speaking countries, to access by internet.

Do you have a favourite (commercial) supplier?

My favourite supplier is Runåbergs Fröer. It's a small Swedish company, growing heirloom varieties. They benefit from the Swedish exception from the seed legislation of the European Union. Adaptive seeds sell seeds for adapting to your cold climate.

I mention these two, being aware they are not the only of their kind. But I guess most will have other companies in mind, and these two deserve more attention from gardeners with short seasons. Both encourage costumers to grow their own seeds.

Do you have books and/or websites that you recommend?

Carol Deppe - Breed Your Own Vegetable Varieties. This book woke me up :-)

Homegrown Goodness is a great forum, with lots of experienced gardeners growing anything with leaves or roots ;-)

Do you have a favourite garden to visit that grows a lot of unusual edibles?

I know a nice lady with a tiny 100 m^2 allotment. She grows a huge crop of vegetables of all kinds in this tiny area. She has an exceptional feeling for intercropping and vertical growing. I'm always breath taken when I step into her garden.

What are your hints and tips for sourcing unusual edibles?

Join your national or regional seed savers. If you find interesting unusual edibles on somebody's blog, they are usually willing to share, provided they have enough seeds to share. Years back, I was desperate for some plants or seeds of the victory onion. Google showed me a Japanese website, just showing the Latin name. It looked like a personal website, there was an email, but the rest was all Japanese signs. I mailed my request, offering seeds of what I had in return. With a robot interpretation we managed to exchange seeds, although we had no language in common. What a wonderful world.

Ian Pearson

I grew up on a Scottish commercial market garden in the '70s, where I suppose I developed the basic gardening skills. In West London I had a small urban back garden, with a small greenhouse, and two nearby allotment plots (closely surrounded by high-rise flats, industrial buildings, and a railway line). I'm interested in sustainable agricultural techniques, and have recently moved to a small farm on the Isle of Wight.

My blog is called Growing Oca: http://oca-testbed.blogspot.co.uk

What unusual edibles do you grow?

Andean tuber crops, edible wild plants, new and heritage varieties of conventional vegetables. Recently, I've been dipping a toe into plant breeding.

How did your interest in unusual edibles develop?

Once a gardener has got to grips with standard cultural techniques and crops, and is putting enough veg on the plate, to me it seems natural to gradually start experimenting with the more unusual, diverse, and challenging vegetables. I always like to be learning something from my garden, and that is an easy situation to achieve if a few new crops are introduced periodically. It's even more of an adventure with crops whose cultivation is poorly documented, and that are rarely grown.

How do you track down your unusual seeds and plants?

I find some can be obtained from specialist suppliers, but more and more I rely on internet seed-swapping. It's an incredibly important, powerful and fast-growing movement that satisfies a need not met by the commercial world.

Do you have a favourite (commercial) supplier?

No, I have two! Agroforestry Research Trust, and Real Seeds.

Do you have books and/or websites that you recommend?

I keep coming back to 'Vegetables' by Roger Phillips & Martyn Rix. Also useful is the Plants for a Future database.

Do you have a favourite garden to visit that grows a lot of unusual edibles?

No. I mean to go to the ART garden someday, and when I do it will probably be my favourite.

What are your hints and tips for sourcing unusual edibles?

Grow a crop of something fairly unusual that you think others will want. Make a good job of it, and save plenty of the best seed/bulbs/tubers/rooted cuttings for trading. Now you have something to swap, join a couple of forums that include seed-swapping groups, and trade away! Growing advice usually comes free. Lots of amateur growers sell their seeds and tubers through eBay.

Frank Van Keirsbilck

I'm gardening in Belgium for about 25 years now, and I'm combining this with my curiosity for unknown edible plants. This is some sort of passion for me, and it takes up lots of time researching and obtaining these plants. The garden is integrated into an orchard, which has lots of old varieties, apples, pears, blackberries, medlar, and so on.... I'm trying to work the ground as little as possible in order not to change the structure of the ground. Compost and fully matured humanure are used as fertiliser, and plants of the Fabaceae [pea and bean] family provide me some more nitrogen.

Providing food for a whole year is easier when you integrate some uncommon edible plants, they can fill up gaps during winter/spring. And moreover, it's a lot healthier if you eat more diversely. Everything is grown in an organic way, no pesticides, no fungicides.... There are some perennial patches, but permaculture is unfortunately very hard over here because of the overwhelming presence of mice. One of my aims is maintaining (and possibly enlarging) the food diversity while it's still possible, too much has disappeared already, and that's a shame!

My website is The Vegetable Garden:
http://www.thevegetablegarden.be

What unusual edibles do you grow?

I have way too many unusual vegetables to list them all, but I do have a specific interest in Andean tubers and roots, which are very promising under Western European circumstances. I'm talking about yacón, oca, mashua, mauka and other plants, some could be the 'potato of future generations' once some more research and more selection has been made.

Every edible plant deserves lots of attention, even if things are weedy (stinging nettles for instance) or very small and easily overlooked (like Shepherd's Needle, *Scandix pecten-veneris)*. All can contribute to a more diverse food palette and to a healthier diet, and bring some more diversity to agriculture as well, although I realise some plants will never reach the stage of becoming a big agricultural crop.

How did your interest in unusual edibles develop?

I moved to a new house some twenty years ago, and there was a nice piece of land that came with it (that actually was one of the reasons for moving over here), and I wanted some herbs. I went to a small local herb nursery where they had some thyme, rosemary, and some other common herbs. But that nursery, small as it was, had a very nice collection of wild plants and some very at that time hard to find edible plants. I bought some crosne (Chinese artichokes, *Stachys affinis)* that day, and got intrigued. I went to the library to find if some more unusual edibles were listed in a book, but I didn't find anything. I went to the botanical garden of Brussels, where I checked their library, and came up with some interesting things, like *Lathyrus tuberosus,* oca, curled mallow.... I got hooked and started to look for these plants, and nowadays I'm still looking for 'new' marvels....

How do you track down your unusual seeds and plants?

I don't have one specific method, I developed a big exchange resource over the years. I'm checking genebanks, I ask friends who travel to look out for something unusual in that area, I check nurseries, I read forums, I'm a member of Seed Savers Exchange and Arche Noah....

Do you have a favourite (commercial) supplier?

No, not really, but some are worthwhile mentioning: Real Seeds in the UK, the German genebank in Gatersleben, Arche Noah in Austria.

Do you have books and/or websites that you recommend?

The most useful book I have is an edible plant encyclopedia: Cornucopia II, a source book of edible plants, which lists thousands of species and varieties. One of the best websites is PFAF, Plants for a Future, but there are other good ones.

Do you have a favourite garden to visit that grows a lot of unusual edibles?

Yes, the botanical garden of Brussels has an amazing collection of unusual edibles, it always surprises me to see the things they grow over there.

What are your hints and tips for sourcing unusual edibles?

Search thoroughly, the internet is a very good searching medium that broadened my vision years ago; ask people where they did get this or that plant, get some useful books if you think you're really interested, visit gardens....

Profile: Mark Diacono

Mark Diacono only came to share his wife's interest in gardening at the beginning of the new millennium. Since moving to Otter Farm in Devon, he has 17 acres to play with, and delights in filling them with edible plants. Mark's particular focus is attempting to grow crops that would otherwise be imported, and he's banking on climate change making some of these plants from warmer climates easier to grow in the future.

What does Mark grow?

Otter Farm is home to pecans, quince, almonds, Szechuan pepper, apricots and a vineyard. Mark has tried his hand at olives, alpine strawberries, blue honeysuckle, Egyptian walking onions, Japanese wineberries, kai lan, autumn olive, medlars, salsify and giant red mustard and quince. He aims to try something new every year.

How did Mark's interest in unusual edibles develop?

After catching the gardening bug and buying the farm, Mark had to decide which plants to grow. Sitting down with Jane Grigson's 'Fruit Book' (because Mark is a foodie at heart), he made a list of what he liked to eat. Although most of the foods he chose were imported, Mark whittled down the list to things that stood a chance of growing here in the future, and his 'Climate Change Farm' was born.

How does Mark source his plants?

Mark is a fan of Jekka McVicar's herb farm and Edulis. He recommends developing a relationship with your favourite suppliers, as they will often give advice on what will grow well in your area - and they may be able to help you find plants that they don't stock themselves.

Mark has also said that he finds the Agroforestry Research Trust very inspiring, and of course they supply plants as well as information.

And Mark now has his own Otter Farm Shop, selling seeds and plants of his favourite varieties.

Hints and tips

If, like Mark, you want to experiment with plants that may fair well in a warmer future, Mark recommends looking out for later-flowering varieties that should be less affected by a cold start in spring. Throughout the Mediterranean region (for example) there are spots with cooler climates, especially those at higher altitudes, with varieties that might be suitable.

And Mark recommends the Japanese wineberry as an easy unusual edible to start with - it's a delicious berry managed in a similar way to blackberries and raspberries.

Mark's books

Mark's book on gourmet unusual edibles, 'A Taste of the Unexpected' was published by Quadrille in September 2010. The American version, 'The Food Lover's Garden: Amazing Edibles You Will Love to Grow and Eat', was published by Timber Press in January 2011.

Mark's next book, 'A Year at Otter Farm' was published by Bloomsbury in June 2014.

Websites

Main: http://www.otterfarm.co.uk

Blog: http://www.otterfarmblog.co.uk

Otter Farm Shop: http://shop.otterfarm.co.uk

Twitter: @MarkDoc

Facebook: https://www.facebook.com/otterfarm

Kate Flint

I had the pleasure of meeting Kate when she came to England for the FoGroBloMe blogger meet-up in 2008, as part of her travels to meet other gardeners. Back then she called South Australia home and was a member of the Hills and Plains Seedsavers (http://hillsandplainsseedsavers.blogspot.com). In March 2010 Kate moved to Hobart, Tasmania, and began writing the tales of The Vegetable Vagabond (http://vegetablevagabond.blogspot.com).

Kate's Edible Water Garden

"Adelaide, the capital of South Australia, is a city of a million or so people, situated at the end of a very long river, The River Murray. All along its length, water from the Murray is taken to supply towns, to irrigate what is the food bowl of Australia and to fill wetlands and billabongs which form the breeding grounds for millions of birds and other wildlife. Barely any water has reached the mouth of the Murray for some years.

The wide River Murray flows slowly through areas of extreme summer heat, so evaporation is high and salts become concentrated by the time it approaches Adelaide. In summer, water is taken from the Murray to supplement Adelaide's dams and there are times when there is not enough. Recently Adelaide and South Australia in general have been subjected to severe summer water restrictions and it was during that time that I began to think of the best ways to use the water allowance to grow food.

When the air temperature soars into the mid 40°C's for weeks at a time, and evaporation is extreme, it is hard to keep yourself hydrated, never mind your withering vegetable garden. In spring I had been shopping at an Asian grocery market when I saw a pot of reeds marked "water chestnuts". I asked the woman about them and she explained that I should submerse the pot of reeds in a tub of water and then, in late autumn the reeds would die down and I should drain the tub and would then be able to harvest water chestnuts from under the soil, like potatoes. I could then save some to replant the following spring.

I was fascinated.... I love water chestnuts and couldn't wait to grow some of my own. So, months later, after weeks of extreme, unbearable summer heat and drought, what was still green and happy in my poor garden? One lone pot of reeds, sitting in a old tub filled with water. I had also thrown in some watercress shoots from the same grocer and these had sprouted and covered the surface of the water, keeping it clear and relatively cool. Topped up with water only occasionally, this little oasis flourished.

So began my love of growing edible water plants; making luxuriant, green leaves and containers of water a cooling and surprisingly water-efficient feature of my summer vegetable garden.

I searched the internet for information but although there was a little, it did not help me find more plants for my water garden at all, since South Australian quarantine laws are very strict. Being a state surrounded by desert, it is happily free of many pests and diseases and movement of any plant matter into the state is understandably restricted. So, back I went to the little Asian grocer and talked some more to the lady whose English was not much better than my Vietnamese. But she got the idea and from time to time I managed to get some edible water plants from her, including yams and kang kong (water spinach).

Every week I bought different Asian greens, not plants, I mean vegetables. I would look up their names and sometimes, if it appeared they were a water plants, I would put a few stems in a vase and see if I could get roots to grow. Sometimes I had wonderful success. I would then plant out the rooted stems into a water-filled tub and see what happened.

It was such a joy to be able to garden in this way right through the heat of summer. I positioned four large tubs such that they were shaded for a couple of hours during the hottest part of the day and it was so wonderful to go out and pick some leaves for lunch, no matter how hot and dry the rest of the garden was.

The bonus was the frogs that arrived from nowhere and took up residence, croaking and singing through the summer nights. The blue-winged dragonflies somehow found my garden too and as the insects increased, so did the native birds and lizards. So, my edible water garden was providing food not just for me but was also providing a little bit of paradise for the wildlife, in a parched land.

There are lots of Asian people in Adelaide, from so many countries and cultures that the food available at markets and in restaurants has to be seen to be believed. But what is sometimes called kang kong by the Vietnamese is called something else by Thai or Chinese people and it is very confusing!

One day in a bookshop I came across Joy Larkcom's "Oriental Vegetables". Joy lists all known names for every vegetable and sorts out what comes from where, how to grow it and even how it is traditionally used in cooking. This book is so wonderful that it has travelled all over the world with me. I recommend it to everyone and hope that by doing so, more people will find some beautiful Asian vegetables to grow, especially now that genuine seed is more readily available and that others in hot, dry climates might seek out plants to grow in water so that gardening in summer will once more bring a smile to their faces and a skip to their step even when temperatures reach into the 40°C's."

Tel Jensen

Tel Jensen lives in Washington State, and blogs about gardening and plants at http://firstchurchofdirt.org/ptblog/blog. Pikkufarm.org is a website dedicated to the land his family has owned for around a hundred years. He used to grow food for a living, but on his own time wants nothing to do with any carrots or beets or parsnips or any of that rot and mostly grows fruit trees and shrubs, with a few self-seeding annuals and an increasing number of perennial vegetables as well.

What unusual edibles do you grow?

I've got a lot of them listed at MyFolia.com. There are some less common strawberries, medlars, mashua, jostaberries, crosne, groundnuts, and a lot more. I like the *Eleagnaceae* family, so I've got a few of those. In the permaculture style, I like plants with multiple uses. I like perennials more than annuals. I like fruit a lot.

How did your interest in unusual edibles develop?

My mom encouraged me to "be myself" growing up, and this normally took the form of her being pleased if I did something weird. Years down the road, I got a job working on a small farm – a great job that I've only just retired from after nine years. A few years into that, I became interested in permaculture after reading an article in the now defunct Clamor magazine. That led me to a permaculture design class at the Bullocks' Homestead where I saw and tasted and used all sorts of plants I had never heard of. That experience opened my eyes to just how much more diverse and delicious a garden could be than the typical veggie patch I had been familiar with, and I've been hooked on finding new (to me) and tasty plants ever since.

How do you track down your unusual seeds and plants?

Eric Toensmeier's *Perennial Vegetables* has been a great inspiration. His list of resources in the back was a good place to start. Internet searches. Seed Savers Exchange. One Green World and Northwoods Nursery in

Molalla, Oregon, USA are great sources of quite a few less common fruit and nut plants from around the world. Raintree Nursery in Morton, Washington, USA is also great. I'm right in between the two. I've traded some plants with folks on MyFolia. Tradewinds Fruit, in California. The appendices in the back of David Jacke's *Edible Forest Gardens* have some great lists of useful plants. Chatting with other permaculturists is always inspiring, too.

Do you have a favourite (commercial) supplier?

Not really. I've probably given more money to Northwoods Nursery than any other place, because I've got a wholesale account there so the prices are much better. They are nice folks, so I'll say they're my favorite. One Green World is the retail outlet for Northwoods, I believe, or Northwoods is the wholesale outlet for One Green World. Or something.

Do you have books and/or websites that you recommend?

Plants for a Future, of course, the book and the website, though the search function isn't so great on the website. I've already mentioned *Perennial Vegetables* and *Edible Forest Gardens.* A browse around https://www.onegreenworld.com and the Raintree Nursery website might be worthwhile.

Do you have a favourite garden to visit that grows a lot of unusual edibles?

The Washington Park Arboretum in Seattle has a lot of great plants. So do the University of Washington's various gardens and greenhouses on campus. The Bullocks' place on Orcas Island is outstanding. Any garden that any of my friends have. A friend from Cameroon grows some crazy stuff in a community garden plot, though she's moving out of town.

What are your hints and tips for sourcing unusual edibles?

I'm actually not very good at this. I would say spending a lot of time with like-minded folks. Offering trades. Join a seed exchange. Learn to speak foreign languages and get agricultural import permits.

Joy Larkcom

Joy Larkcom is a garden writer and has specialised in vegetables for over 40 years. With her husband, Donald Pollard, Joy ran an experimental organic market garden in Suffolk, supplying a wholefood shop in London, local restaurants and other outlets. Their speciality was bags of mixed salads, which they called 'Saladini'. Joy and Donald discovered many of the plants they included during a year's travel on the continent, with their young children, in 1976 and 77.

Joy has always been interested in the concept of making a kitchen garden beautiful as well as productive, and has established several 'potagers' which encompass this idea. Joy and Donald have now retired to West Cork in Ireland, and are growing on a much smaller scale for themselves, largely in raised beds made from recycled plastic.

What unusual edibles do you grow?

The most unusual vegetables we grow are Asiatic in origin, and mainly grown for use in the winter months. These would include the many hardy Asiatic mustards, mizuna, mibuna, the mild flavoured 'February orchid' (*Orychophragmus violaceus),* and a range of pak chois. We always grow a selection of tomatoes which we consider the best flavoured, as well as a few of the more unusual salads plants such as summer and winter purslane. Our favourite heirloom vegetable is the Crimson Flowered broad bean.

How and why did your interest in unusual edibles develop?

My interest in unusual edibles probably dates back to my student days studying horticulture at Wye College, London University. I once arranged an exhibition of what were then considered unusual vegetables - such as scorzonera and salsify. Then our year travelling in Europe, 'The Grand Vegetable Tour' we called it, brought other vegetables to my attention, particularly salad vegetables and the use of wild plants. After that I became very interested in the huge range of unknown, mainly leafy, oriental vegetables and went to Asia, the USA and Canada to study their cultivation.

How do you track down your unusual plants?

I often found interesting new vegetable varieties in seed trials, such as those organised by Elsoms Seeds and Tozers Seeds.

Do you have a favourite commercial supplier?

I mainly use the UK retail mail order seed companies, as they all now offer some of the unusual vegetables I am interested in. In the past I worked closely with Suffolk Herbs seed company, to introduce the Italian salad plants, such as the chicories, and the colourful lettuces such as 'Lollo', which we had discovered on the Continent. Over the years I also worked closely with Tozer Seeds, and CN Seeds, who were interested in new introductions.

What are your hints and tips for sourcing unusual edibles?

Probably today the web is the best source for sourcing seed of unusual edibles, as it gives contacts in the USA as well as the UK and Europe. Most seed companies now have their catalogues online. I still prefer to use an old fashioned 'hard' copy of a seed catalogue in selecting seed that I want.

Where can we find out more about your work?

I have put years of research and experiment into the books I have written, and the following four are still in print: Grow Your Own Vegetables, The Organic Salad Garden, Oriental Vegetables, Creative Vegetable Gardening.

My final book, 'Just Vegetating', was published in spring 2012. This is a collection of articles written in the last 40 years, woven together with reminiscences, updates and descriptions of our 1976/77 Grand Vegetable Tour.

Hedvig Murray

Hedvig Murray is part of the Get Growing project
(http://www.getgrowing.org.uk) - a social enterprise that trains people
to grow food (including heritage varieties) in their own homes.

What unusual edibles do you grow?

Daffodil garlic, purple chilli plants, red orache, lemongrass, cape
gooseberries, Nepalese cherry tomatoes, pink garlic from Abruzzo (from
a Slow Food grower at the Slow Food Salone de Gusto). Heritage
tomatoes, lettuces, peas, beans, amaranth, kale. Next year I'm going to
grow lettuce asparagus.

How and why did your interest in unusual edibles develop?

As a young girl, I made pansies "kiss" and realised they produced
flowers that had different colours. An interest in unusual edible flowers
developed then and there. Just after this my mum gave me a book
called Linnea's Windowsill Garden and I started growing things like
avocados - not that common for young girls in the 1980s. I'd go with my
mum to allotments and hear the old boys tell her about different ways
of growing and learning about the old plants in our garden. So I've
always seen gardening as experimental, and growing unusual edibles
certainly feels like it is a big old experiment and all the more exciting
because of that.

In my early twenties I became increasingly aware about the issues
around biodiversity and intellectual property rights. In 2006 I went on a
course at Vandana Shiva's educational centre near Dehra Dun, India and
was amazed to learn more about the varieties they were growing and
defending from patents. I was horrified that what I did very naturally as
a child could be illegal, and that growers the world over might be unable
to breed, grow, save and exchange the seeds of the plants they have
been developing. It became clear how plants have a heritage – both
with specific growers and geographical areas.

When I came back to the UK, I found out about the Heritage Seed Library and loved the idea of keeping the varieties alive through growing rather than in banks. I love reading or imagining the stories about the growers and the regions. Through doing community gardening in London I came across all manner of unusual things that people had grown or wanted to grow. Now, through the work of the Brighton Permaculture Trust, I am learning more about local apple varieties - which for someone who has travelled all her life is fascinating.

How do you track down your unusual seeds and plants?

I don't search out plants, but come across them. I find out about them on blogs, websites, on visits, from friends.

Do you have a favourite (commercial) supplier?

HSL (pseudo commercial)

Do you have books and/or websites (or other sources of information) that you recommend?

http://emmacooper.org!

What are your hints and tips for sourcing unusual edibles?

Follow your passions - if you do that you usually end up with something unusual. That's what happens to me anyway. And don't be afraid to ask for cuttings/seeds. People who are passionate about growing unusual stuff are usually surprised and delighted to share.

Dave Richards

Dave discovered the work of Lawrence Hills, WWOOFed and spent 10 years working with unemployed youth on city farms in Bristol. An interest in sustainable development was sparked by a year spent travelling overland to Indonesia and since 1989 Dave has worked at Reading International Solidarity Centre (RISC), an educational charity that aims to raise awareness of global issues. There he is responsible for the roof garden and curriculum development in the outdoor classroom, particularly as a tool for exploring global citizenship.

http://www.risc.org.uk/gardens

http://www.food4families.org.uk

http://www.globalgardens.org.uk

What unusual edibles do you grow?

Our choice of plants was determined by the purpose of the garden, to demonstrate the importance of plants in human history and show how forest gardens are a valuable approach to low maintenance food growing. So our plants have to work together as a designed eco-system and tell stories, as well as taste, smell and look good. We now have over 185 different species and varieties of useful plant in about 200 m^2. They include heritage varieties of English fruit trees as well as trees, shrubs and herbaceous perennials from the world's temperate regions.

How and why did your interest in unusual edibles develop?

My parents began my interest in gardening. My Chinese mum was a great believer in pee power and my dad passed on his 'Dig for Victory' skills.

RISC decided to create an edible outdoor classroom on a leaking flat roof. The design emerged from brain storming sessions with Paul Barney, a local permaculture designer. In 2002 forest gardens were still relatively unknown, so Paul's initial planting list was a bit of a mystery.

Now that these have matured into a really wonderful space, Japanese wineberry, Turkish rocket and chokeberry have become staples of my designs for school gardens.

How do you track down your unusual seeds and plants?

The Agroforestry Trust has a fantastic selection of plants that are especially useful for forest gardens, but are sold out early in the autumn. We owe Martin Crawford a huge debt for introducing useful perennial plants from all over the world, including more productive cultivars of wild species.

Do you have a favourite supplier?

The Organic Gardening Catalogue has a reasonable selection of more familiar seeds and plants.

Chiltern Seeds have a vast selection of common and unusual seeds. Crûg Farm Nursery have a superb selection of plants from East Asia. Kore Wild Fruit Nursery also has an excellent range of unusual fruit that is especially good for forest gardeners.

Do you have books and/or websites (or other sources of information) that you recommend?

Martin Crawford, Creating a Forest Garden

Simon Hickmott, Growing Unusual Vegetables

Sally Cunningham, Asian Vegetables

Eric Toensmeier, Perennial Vegetables

Do you have a favourite garden to visit that grows a lot of unusual edibles?

The Agroforestry Research Trust.

Profile: Eric Toensmeier

What does Eric grow?

A lot of perennial vegetables! The idea being that perennial vegetables require far less care and attention than annual vegetables, yet are still productive. Eric has moved beyond the familiar perennial edibles (rhubarb, asparagus and artichokes) to find a lot more (over 100 are mentioned in his book) that can be grown in North America and similar climate zones. He also has an interest in Native American edibles.

How did Eric's interest in unusual edibles develop?

He says he has spent most of his adult life exploring the edible and useful plants of the world, so he must have caught the bug very young!

How does Eric source his plants?

Eric points out that it can be difficult to source seeds for perennial edibles, and that the only solution is to ask suppliers for them if you want to grow them. If there is enough demand they will begin to appear in catalogues.

Hints and tips

Newly planted perennials usually follow the 'sleep, creep and leap' model - doing very little in their first year, growing slowly in their second and then really getting into their stride in their third year once their root systems have become established. At that point you may find you have an excess of vegetation. Eric's suggestions are to turn it into eggs and fertile compost via some backyard chickens and to toast marshmallows over a fire disposing of woody stems!

Books

'Perennial Vegetables: From Artichokes to Zuiki Taro, A Gardener's Guide to Over 100 Delicious and Easy to Grow Edibles' was published by Chelsea Green in in October 2007 and is now also available for Kindle.

Eric collaborated with Dave Jacke to write the two-volume 'Edible Forest Gardens' (about forest gardening in temperate climates), both published by Chelsea Green in April 2006.

Chelsea Green released Eric's latest book 'Paradise Lot: Two Plant Geeks, One-Tenth of an Acre, and the Making of an Edible Garden Oasis in the City' in June 2013.

Websites

http://www.perennialsolutions.org

http://www.edibleforestgardens.com

http://perennialvegetables.org

Owen Smith

Owen Smith founded an independent seed company, Future Foods, devoted to weird and wonderful edibles that deserved a second chance. Owen later handed over the reins to Simon Hickmott, and unfortunately the company ceased trading a few years ago. The results of Owen's 'root crop research and ruminations' can be found on his blog, Radix (http://radix4roots.blogspot.com) and you can find him on Twitter (as @Rhizowen) and Facebook (https://www.facebook.com/groups/141198905918483).

What unusual edibles do you grow?

At the moment I'm concentrating my efforts on obtaining and evaluating the potential of alternative root crops, simply because these are among the easiest and most productive plants for home gardeners in terms of calories produced. My aim is to use these plants to produce a resilient, high yielding, disease resistant polyculture in association with the good old potato. With a bit of persistence and experimentation (collaborators welcome!) this might possibly be achieved; given the erratic nature of our weather lately, this sort of cropping system could provide a useful backup when grain crops fail. Among the crops I am experimenting with are oca (*Oxalis tuberosa*), hopniss (*Apios americana*) mauka (*Mirabilis expansa*) and mashua (*Tropaeolum tuberosum*). I have managed to obtain viable seeds of both oca and mauka, which suggests that breeding improved varieties for our climate and latitude is perfectly feasible. The anarchist in me wants to break the hegemony of the Eurasian crop diversity centre by scouring the world's cool temperate and maritime regions for edible plants which are better adapted to our peculiar (in world terms) climate. Search globally, sow locally.

I am a fully paid-up phytonerd (with the scars to prove it) so I continue to experiment with other plants in a desultory way as time and space allows. I'm working on breeding hardier chillies, crossing *Cucurbita* species in an attempt to produce a perennial, cold tolerant squash and trialling pretty much anything that takes my fancy. In the past I've worked my way through a range of unusual fruits, nuts and grains. It's too late to stop now.

How and why did your interest in unusual edibles develop?

I've been passionate about plants since early childhood (I have the photographic evidence) and I love to get acquainted with plants. I've also found eating to be something of an enduring interest. Combining these two strands led me to start Future Foods back in the early 1990s. There are so many edible plants whose merits have not yet been discovered; once you've got hold of the plants and grown them, there's so much to learn about how to adapt them to our cooking styles and make something delicious from them. I have to confess that I'm still struggling with the latter in some cases! The biggest problem is, that as I work my way through the list of suitable plants, I keep discovering new ones. Oh well, researching them helps while away those dark winter evenings.

How do you track down your unusual seeds and plants?

There's no denying what a boon the internet has been to the hardened phytonerd. A bit of legwork will often yield up suppliers for some fairly obscure stuff. I'm a member of various forums which often lead me to sources of the plants I'm looking for. Sometimes phone calls or emails put me in contact with the right person. Persistence usually pays off eventually: it took me 15 years to track down seeds of mauka (*Mirabilis expansa*) for example. I'm glad I kept at it, because it's a cracker. More than anything else, I'm delighted to have been able to share its seeds with other plant enthusiasts: the cycle continues.

Do you have a favourite supplier?

Suppliers come and go (look at Future Foods!) but I often use Real Seeds, Chiltern Seeds, SSE and you can pick up some very interesting stuff on eBay too.

Do you have books and/or websites (or other sources of information) that you recommend?

My copy of Cornucopia (now 20 years old) was a great source when it came out, but it's getting a little out of date now. Likewise the SSE inventories, which I've had almost as long. I enjoy the Homegrown Goodness forums for specialised information and I can't resist plugging the Radix Root Crops Facebook page, which is yielding up plenty of new and interesting information.

Do you have a favourite garden to visit that grows a lot of unusual edibles?

The Eden Project is just down the road and is nice to visit at off peak times. I particularly like the monkey puzzle grove, which is going great guns, although I'm not sure whether the trees are going to produce any nuts any time soon. Shame, because they're tasty.

What are your hints and tips for sourcing unusual edibles?

We are currently living at the best time ever for amateurs to source unusual plant material – the range available is quite remarkable. While I celebrate this abundance, I feel we should act responsibly by not transferring plants illegally; nor should we try and appropriate crop plants developed by others for our own personal gain through claiming restrictive intellectual property rights. I am of the opinion that citizen-led research and breeding projects could yield up some excellent new crops that will provide gardeners in with diverse flavours and nutrition.

Simon Suter

Simon Suter's photo blog (http://maisiethecat.blogspot.co.uk) shares luscious photos from his garden and others.

What unusual edibles do you grow?

Perennial /biennial veg: Japanese Parsley, Egyptian tree onions, sea kale.

Annual veg: Salsify (black & white), L'agretto, heritage tomatoes (over 20 varieties), Chilli (more than 10 varieties), mouse melon, chicory, pumpkins and the like.

Tubers - Oca, Ulloco, various heritage spuds (Belle de Fontenay, Shetland Back, Salad Blue, etc.), Sweet Potato

Fruit - Chilean Guava, alpine strawberries, blueberry, nectarines

Other - hops, Szechuan pepper

Some are grown for novelty (i.e. not a large crop); others are certainly used in full in the kitchen.

How did your interest in unusual edibles develop?

Not sure; I have being growing veg for many years. Recently expanded with an allotment. Always willing to try something new.

How do you track down your unusual seeds and plants?

Various - web (eBay has proved surprisingly useful), plant fairs, word of mouth.

Do you have a favourite (commercial) supplier?

Seeds of Italy for general stuff. Other niche suppliers include Simpsons Seeds (chilli & toms), Seaspring seeds (mix of veg), Real Seeds, Agroforesty Research Trust, Edulis.

Do you have books and/or websites that you recommend?

Toensmeier - Perennial Vegetables, Christopher Lloyd - Gardener Cook, Simpsons (see seed suppliers) Tomato & Chilli books.

What are your hints and tips for sourcing unusual edibles?

Most people who are daft enough to try growing weird things are more than happy to share their interest and plants with others!

Alison Tindale

Alison Tindale grows perennial vegetable plants in East Yorkshire for sale online at The Backyard Larder (http://backyardlarder.co.uk) - the idea being that perennial vegetables are always there, store-cupboard ingredients alive and growing in your backyard! The plants are also very much of interest to people developing forest gardens - farms of the future perhaps? She blogs at http://backyardlarder.blogspot.co.uk.

What unusual edibles do you grow?

I have two allotments and a tiny backyard and as well as conventional veg I am growing perennial kale, sea kale, Good King Henry, sorrels, comfrey, skirret, scorzonera, buck's horn plantain, tree onions, daylilies.

My plans just now are to carry on propagating plants in my backyard, source new things as and when I can afford to (I am looking for a Mediterranean wild salad plant just now called *Reichardia picroides* - apparently like a dandelion without the bitterness and also slug-proof), grow a collection of edible tubers like oca and mashua and to grow some wild vegetables - perhaps bush or tufted vetch to give a few tiny peas.

How did your interest in unusual edibles develop?

Along with my husband Stew, I'd like to be living the self-sufficient life. If I could do that in a way which helps to make food growing easier (especially for people with busy lifestyles) and in a way which nourishes the planet, well that would be great.

Do you have a favourite (commercial) supplier?

The Agroforestry Research Trust supplies what others have never heard of!

Do you have books and/or websites that you recommend?

I love the Plants for a Future database - what a cornucopia of vital information! For my education, putting me in touch with people committed to finding wonderful new ways of doing things, I go to the Permaculture UK forum (http://www.epfsolutions.org.uk/forum).

What are your hints and tips for sourcing unusual edibles?

I garden on a shoestring so swap sites are proving a real bonus - e.g. Garden SwapShop.

Carl and Debs Legge

Carl and Debs Legge live on the stunning – but windy – Llyn Peninsula in Wales. They are developing their smallholding along permaculture lines, with a forest garden alongside the vegetable patch. Both foodies at heart, Carl is a wizard in the kitchen. He shares his culinary creations on his blog (http://www.carllegge.com) and his first book – The Permaculture Kitchen – was published by Permanent Publications in spring 2014.

What unusual edibles do you grow?

We grow perennial/forest garden type edibles of all sorts that we think might grow here in North Wales. We now have loads, the list would be huge.

How did your interest in unusual edibles develop?

When we moved to our smallholding in 1997, we bought a copy of 'The Alternative Kitchen Garden: An A to Z' and started with the Heritage Seed Library. They sparked our interest. It's your fault, Emma!

How do you track down your unusual seeds and plants?

Via friends on Twitter (Owen Smith is one of the main culprits), the Real Seed Company and the Agroforestry Research Trust.

Do you have a favourite (commercial) supplier?

The Real Seed Company.

Do you have books and/or websites that you recommend?

Owen's blog (radix4roots.blogspot.co.uk) is a mine of useful information. EmmaCooper.org is useful.

Martin Crawford's books *Perennial Vegetables* and *Creating a Forest Garden.* The Agroforestry Research Trust's quarterly newsletter is great.

Pfaf.org is indispensable.

Alys Fowler's books *The Thrifty Forager* and *Abundance* are excellent.

We have a 1990 copy of Elphinstone & Langley's *The Green Gardener's Handbook*, that we love to use.

What are your hints and tips for sourcing unusual edibles?

Twitter is a resource full of experts and keen amateurs. Join in, be friendly and be prepared to share information.

Profile: James Wong

James Wong is a real plant geek, with an MSc in Ethnobotany from the University of Kent. He spent his childhood in Malaysia and Singapore, and his research has taken him across the globe, including highland Ecuador, China and Java. He presented two series of a BBC television programme on herbal remedies, called "Grow Your Own Drugs" (plus a Christmas special!), and now makes regular appearances on Countryfile.

What does James grow?

In James' opinion, although the kind of people growing fruit and vegetables has changed significantly since the Second World War and the Dig for Victory campaign, the advice handed out in gardening magazines and books hasn't kept pace. James thinks we would get a larger financial reward for our gardening efforts if we stopped growing the allotment staples we're used to (which are cheap to buy, in season) and concentrated on the more modern additions to our diet that are far more expensive and hard to come by.

He recommends trying sweet potatoes, cocktail kiwis, saffron, wasabi and stevia. On his website he also champions the Tasmanian pepper bush, and 'electric buttons'.

Hints and tips

As well as advising us to liven up our allotments, James wants us to keep an eye out for exciting edible house plants. Apparently Miracle berries, although large plants in nature, can start fruiting when they are just 30 cm tall (around 2 years old) and don't mind being kept indoors in a pot. After a recent visit to the international HortiFair in Amsterdam (a commercial horticultural expo), James recommends keeping an eye out for cinnamon, vanilla orchids, green tea and coffee plants - all coming to a windowsill near you soon!

James' books

James' two books to accompany the Grow Your Own Drugs series were published by Collins - 'Grow Your Own Drugs: Easy Recipes for Natural Remedies and Beauty Treats' in 2009 and 'Grow Your Own Drugs: A Year With James Wong' in 2010. Both deal more with using your harvests than growing the plants.

'James Wong's Homegrown Revolution' was published in September 2012 and Suttons brought out a new range of seeds for unusual edibles to go with the book.

Websites:

Main: http://www.jameswong.co.uk

Twitter: @botanygeek

CHAPTER THREE

Heritage and heirloom plant varieties

If you're looking for something more unusual to grow, then heritage (or heirloom) vegetables are a good place to start - they are old-fashioned varieties of familiar plants. They are grown and used in the same way as their modern compatriots, but are undeniably different.

A heritage variety is one that used to be commonly grown, but which has fallen out of favour. The obvious examples are commercial seed varieties that have been dropped from sale because they have been replaced by new, 'improved' and more profitable varieties. Heritage veg can also include local varieties - grown for generations in small geographical areas to which they were well suited (although with climate change they may be becoming less so).

National seed laws may prohibit the sale of these varieties - here in Europe we have the EU seed laws that prohibit the sale of vegetable seed varieties that haven't been included on one of the national lists. To be registered on the list is expensive; seed companies allow registrations of older varieties to lapse in order to save money. Heritage seed suppliers can get around the prohibitions by not selling their wares; what you pay for is a membership to their club, and your fee entitles you to the seeds you want. The French seed organisation Association Kokopelli has fallen foul of the law on several occasions over the years. Bifurcated Carrots (http://bifurcatedcarrots.eu) is a good blog to follow for commentary on the political side of seed supply.

Modern seed varieties tend to be bred with farmers in mind - commercial production is where the profits lie. As gardeners we are expected to use the same seeds, but the agricultural benefits of uniformity, a long shelf-life and short harvest windows are less of a boon in the kitchen garden. Gardeners and cooks prefer varieties selected for their flavour, and a longer harvest window that prevents gluts and shortages (unless they want the bulk in one go for canning and preserving). F1 varieties are standardised, a benefit some gardeners appreciate, but they are no good for seed-saving as their offspring will be variable. For that reason alone, many gardeners prefer to grow 'open-pollinated' heirlooms.

The range of heirloom varieties available is spectacular. Each variety has its own advantages and disadvantages; some will flourish in your climate and soil, others will not be at their best in your conditions. Many have their own story to tell; there are far too many for me to mention even a fraction here, but these are some of the more memorable ones I have encountered.

Sub Arctic Plenty Tomato

Sub Arctic Plenty is a tomato variety that was developed to fruit well and ripen properly in Greenland - far north of its homeland. Greenland has a short, cool summer and Sub Arctic Plenty ripens well outside in the UK and similar zones. It produces golf-ball sized, red tomatoes that have (to my mind, but I am not a tomato expert) a good flavour. I found it made a good tomato for juicing; the chickens always appreciated being given the resulting pulp as a treat. Mind you, I have also heard them described as a tomato for people who don't like tomatoes!

Sub Arctic Plenty is a determinate plant - it grows as a bush. Indeterminate tomatoes here in the UK require lavish amounts of training and pruning to produce a crop in our short summer season; I have read that tomatoes elsewhere are a less troublesome crop, and can be confined to neat cages or allowed to sprawl.

Sub Arctic Plenty has gone from commercial variety to heirloom and is making its way back into the seed catalogues, and so is now very easy to source.

To produce a good crop in a short season, tomatoes are usually sown indoors (very often with a little heat to promote rapid germination) in late winter. They then have to be coddled indoors until the risk of frost has passed and they can be hardened off and planted outside. In between times, they can get leggy from lack of light on windowsills (actually a combination of the warm temperatures and low light levels, so moving them to a cooler spot might help), but when you're potting them on or planting them out you can plant them nice and deep and bury the stems right up to the lower leaves, which at least makes them more stable.

Tomatoes need a regular supply of water (which is what makes their cultivation in grow bags so tricky) throughout their lives; irregular watering when they're fruiting can cause blossom end rot (where the bottoms of the tomatoes go nasty) or splitting. A high potash feed is given regularly once they start flowering, to promote heavy crops.

Blight is a big problem in the UK, where we regularly encounter 'Smith Periods' in late summer when warm, humid weather encourages the growth of blight spores. Blight is a disease (caused by a fungus-like organism) that rapidly demolishes tomato (and potato) plants; infected fruit won't keep for long, but is safe to eat. I am not aware of any heritage tomato varieties that are considered to be blight-resistant (although that doesn't mean there are any). If you have real problems with blight then modern varieties are one solution; confining yourself to the early-fruiting cherry tomato varieties is another - they tend to crop before blight sets in.

There are probably more heirloom tomato varieties than one person could possibly hope to grow in a lifetime, ranging from tiny cherries through to gigantic beefsteaks and in most of the colours of the rainbow. Whichever variety you choose, consider underplanting (or interplanting) your tomatoes with dwarf marigolds (*Tagetes*, not *Calendula*) - their distinctive smells help to ward off whitefly.

Crimson-flowered broad bean

The crimson-flowered broad bean has become the poster child of the heritage seed movement. Once you've grown it, you can see why - it's an absolutely stunning plant, and wouldn't look out of place in the flower bed. It is truly an edimental. It's grown in the same way as other broad beans, sown in the autumn (or late winter in nastier climates) for an early spring crop. Broad bean flowers have a lovely scent, only ever appreciated by gardeners as you have to bend in close to pick it up. And they're a valuable source of food for bees early in the spring; so despite the fact that the flowers themselves are edible you should refrain from eating them all. The plants are fruitful and the beans themselves are tasty, although smaller and less regular than modern strains.

While you're down on your knees, weeding the beans or taking in their scent, have a look at their stems - they're square. Broad beans are a thoroughly useful plant, and field beans are often grown as a green manure to fix nitrogen into the soil (although they need the support of the right soil bacteria to do so, and how much nitrogen remains in the soil if the crop is removed is a moot point).

Broad beans are attractive to rodents when sown in the ground, so consider that a possibility if yours fail to come up. Sowing in pots or modules and planting them out is one solution; young plants also need protection from slugs. Once they're growing strongly they're immune to most pests, but tend to attract blackfly. If you pinch out the leafy tops once the plants have reached their final height then that is a big step to keeping them blackfly-free and gives you a nice leafy green to have for dinner.

The crimson-flowered broad bean is another variety that was once popular, fell from commercial use and is now reappearing in the standard plant catalogues. Although it is still not widely available, it's not too hard to source seeds. There is some variability in the seed stock; if you want to save your own seeds then make sure you 'rogue out' any plants that look different (e.g. the ones that don't have particularly crimson flowers).

Vitelotte potatoes

I haven't personally grown this variety, but the Vitelotte is a blue potato. Very blue. And it stays blue after it's cooked, so if you really fancy eating blue mashed potatoes then this one is worth a try. But apparently the colour stains, so be careful! The colour comes from the anthocyanin content, one of those antioxidants we're all supposed to eat more of, so you could have superfood spuds.

Vitelotte is a maincrop potato. It is becoming more widely available, along with other heritage potato varieties, as the last few years have seen the development of microplants and minitubers. These are created under sterile conditions in a laboratory (by tissue culture, not some horrific feat of genetic engineering) and can therefore be supplied as disease-free specimens for gardeners.

Microplants tend to produce small crops in the first year, and the idea is then to save your tubers for replanting the following year. Minitubers are a step up in that process and should produce normal crops. The problem with saving your own tubers and replanting them in future years is that you can't guarantee that they haven't picked up a disease (blight is obvious and leads infected tubers to rot, but viruses are more stealthy) that will be carried on to future generations and cause a lack of vigour and less abundant crops. That doesn't mean that it's impossible, just that it's something many amateur gardeners wouldn't want to attempt. You could also buy a packet of heritage spuds from the supermarket (sold as upmarket, gourmet choices) and leave those sprouting on the windowsill all winter for planting in spring; the advantage of that method is that you can buy enough, relatively cheaply, to eat some and see whether you like it first.

Heritage potato varieties are numerous. The easiest way to get your hands on a good selection is to go along to a Potato Day - they are organised throughout the UK in February and are no doubt becoming a global phenomenon. Many of them are combined with seed swaps and fairs that are a one-stop-shop for all your heritage seed needs.

Cherokee Trail of Tears French bean

This climbing French bean (pole bean in US parlance) is meant to be the one that the Cherokee took with them on their 'Trail of Tears' - their forced march across America as they were displaced from their homeland. It has become one of the enduring stories of the heirloom movement, and a much-loved bean for many people. The Real Seeds team plant it for their own use, as well as their seed catalogue, and report it to be both prolific and cropping over a long period.

Although they require a bit more effort in terms of support, climbing French beans tend to crop over a longer period than dwarf French beans and are able to make use of vertical space - making them a good choice in small gardens. They have become less popular in modern times due to the difficulties of mechanical harvesting - dwarf French beans are easier to produce commercially.

The diversity of heritage French beans (both dwarf and climbing) is immense. Many people effectively collect them; you can choose different heights and cropping times. There are yellow pods and purple pods and different coloured flowers. They are bred to be eaten as green beans, or shelled beans, or dried beans for storage. And the beans themselves come in a beautiful array of colours and patterns. I know of more than a few people who find them so lovely that they stroke them like pets.

Asparagus kale

When I first joined the Heritage Seed Library, it was out of season. The catalogues are sent out in December each year, and orders are taken right through until March. If you join after that you have to wait, but they sent me a free packet of Asparagus Kale to help pass the time. What they didn't do was send me the catalogue or any instructions on how to grow it, which may explain why I have yet to successfully do so. That and the fact that the brassica family isn't my favourite - either to grow or eat.

Like all kales, asparagus kale is a hardy plant for which the seed is sown in spring with an eye to harvests through the following winter. But asparagus kale isn't grown primarily for its leaves; when spring comes around it sends up flowering shoots that are reputed to taste like asparagus. It's one of those seasonal treats you completely miss out on unless you grow your own.

The problem with most brassicas, heirloom or not, is that they take up a lot of space for a very long time. In that sense they make ideal crops for an allotment, where they are fairly low maintenance crops and can feed you through the 'hungry gap' in early spring when there's plenty growing but not much ready for harvest. However, they fall prey to pests and diseases. Winter brassicas need netting against pigeons, and staking against wind rock. In mild weather they can be riddled with whitefly; during the summer months they need very fine netting to keep off the cabbage white butterflies whose eggs would turn into voracious caterpillars. Club root is a pernicious disease that stunts brassicas and is both easily transmitted (it is soil borne) and almost impossible to eradicate.

In my (smallish) garden I therefore tend to stick to the smaller brassica species, in particular the oriental vegetables that are smaller and more quickly grown. Mind you, I am partial to purple sprouting broccoli and have on occasions found that worth the effort; there are currently no heirloom varieties of that because until recently there were no varieties beyond 'early' and 'late', although that is now changing.

However, there are plenty of people who find brassicas more inspiring, and plenty of heirloom kales to go around. If you want something spectacular, keep an eye out for Jersey or Walking Stick kale, a plant that grows a stem long (and hard) enough to use as a walking stick. I'm told it tastes pretty good, too. A kale variety I have adopted (but not yet grown) is Uncle Bert's Purple; although it had nothing to do with him I chose it in memory of my (great) Uncle Bert, who was himself a product of a bygone age - a true gentleman and much missed.

Tutankhamen's Peas

There is an enduring urban legend that pea seeds found in Tutankhamen's tomb in the 1800s were not only still viable but have been handed down since then in the form of several varieties with evocative names involving Tutankhamen or mummies. In truth, the oldest known seed to have been successfully germinated was only about 2,000 years old and was a Judean date palm (according to Wikipedia) and Egyptian tomb peas were probably just some clever marketing to take advantage of the European Eygyptomania of the time. You can therefore safely grow these varieties without the risk of falling foul of the mummy's curse! The Tutanhkamen's Pea offered by the Heritage Seed Library is a nice tall variety with white flowers, and easily picked pea pods with sweet tasting peas.

Heritage peas do tend to be a lot taller than modern varieties, although there are some notable exceptions. The Half Pint Pea rarely tops 30 cm and is perfect for growing in windowboxes, although when I tried it I found it a little harder to keep happy than its larger relatives. I have better luck with the parsley pea, which is equally dinky and has stunning foliage that closely resembles curly parsley.

Heritage pea varieties come in different flower and pod colours as well as a range of heights. Round seeds are hardier and can be sown into the autumn for late crops, or in early spring. Wrinkle-seeded varieties are sown in spring for summer harvests, and are theoretically sweeter, although a lot will depend on the variety you choose. Mice love pea seeds, and slugs love seedlings, but the biggest problem for most pea plants is the dreaded pea moth that makes its appearance during the summer months - maggoty peas are the result. You can time your crops to avoid the peak pea moth season, or keep the plants covered in fleece for protection. After a bad attack it is best to avoid growing peas for a couple of years to allow the pest population to die off.

Forgotten Vegetables

While it is easy to see how vegetables from other countries may never have found their way onto our plates, and why heritage varieties may have fallen from modern commercial favour, there are vegetables and fruits that were once common but are now largely forgotten. These aren't wild plants, languishing by the roadside waiting for their virtues to be rediscovered, but cultivated ones that for some reason are no longer popular.

Given their long history of vegetable gardening (including their beautiful *pótagers* and the famously intensive market gardens of Paris in the 19th century), it is perhaps not surprising that the topic of forgotten vegetables seems to resonate most strongly in the French. It is often easier to find relevant information (although harder to read the results!) if you search for 'les légumes retrouvés' or 'les légumes oubliés'.

One of the reasons these vegetables have fallen out of favour is that they were used as 'famine foods', sustaining populations through hard times they would prefer to forget. This is particularly true in parts of Europe where food crops were confiscated for military use during World War II - the more obvious and common vegetables would have been the first to go, leaving these less familiar species as the only things left to support the civilian population. With the current emphasis on resilience, and a perceived need for survival crops in some communities, this ability to 'hide in plain sight' (perhaps in the flower bed) may still be considered an advantage.

These vegetables may also be less convenient to prepare and cook, but I think their subsequent rediscovery belies the belief that they were replaced by tastier alternatives - the French are turning back to them as gourmet choices.

Salsify and scorzonera

Salsify and scorzonera are usually mentioned together, because the edible roots they produce look and taste similar, and the plants are grown in the same way. But they are different species - salsify is *Tragopogon porrifolius,* whilst scorzonera is *Scorzonera hispanica.*

Salsify is often called the vegetable oyster, because its roots are supposed to have an oyster-like flavour although I suspect nobody would be fooled. The long roots are pale and a bit like carrots - they are mild and sweet and when young can be eaten raw. Mature roots are better cooked. Traditionally a winter food, any roots left in the ground in spring will produce a flush of edible foliage.

Scorzonera roots are much darker, often nearly black, and cylindrical. It seems they have a much thicker skin than carrots, and are best cooked in it and then peeled (although opinions are divided). They may stain hands, and certainly rapidly darken when exposed to the air and so peeled roots need to be kept under water or sprinkled with lemon juice. Like Jerusalem artichokes, scorzonera roots have a high inulin content, but they can be left in the ground for two seasons without them becoming woody, which makes for a larger harvest. And like salsify, plants left in the ground produce edible leaves in spring and Martin Crawford treats scorzonera as a perennial for this purpose, rather than lift the roots.

Salsify and/or scorzonera seeds make an appearance in most catalogues - the variety names they are given, 'Mammoth', 'Maxima' and 'Russian Giant' obviously favour the 'bigger is better' school of thought when it comes to roots. Seed has a short shelf-life, and it is best to buy (or save) new seed every year. Both vegetables are reasonably common on allotments, but you would be hard-pressed to buy roots commercially.

Skirret

Skirret, *Sium sisarum,* is a little harder to come by. It's another perennial grown for its roots, but can make a larger plant than salsify and scorzonera and grow up to a metre tall. And rather than send down single roots, it grows a crown from which the edible roots are formed. If you harvest the storage roots carefully, leaving the crown and its growing points intact, then it should be possible to persuade the plant to continue growing. Plants can also be propagated by division.

The small roots can be eaten raw or cooked, but tend to have a woody core that is inedible and needs to be removed (although Farmer Scrub found that this is not always the case, http://farmerscrub.blogspot.co.uk/2010/05/crop-summary-skirret-sium-sisarum.html). Roots can be eaten after more than a year of cultivation, so skirret would seem like an interesting, hardy, low-maintenance and almost perennial root crop that would be worth trying if you have the space. Roots can be left in the ground until needed, and (as for many root crops) become sweeter over time as starches are converted into sugars in cold weather.

Allowing skirret to flower does not affect the final yield, so it is also possible to save your own seed. Seed is, however, slow to germinate. Soaking it in water overnight before sowing could speed things up considerably; stratifying seeds should also ensure success.

Cardoon

The globe artichoke (*Cynara cardunculus* var. *scolymus*) makes a statuesque addition to the vegetable garden if you have the space - they grow up to 150 cm tall and look like giant thistles. The unopened flower buds provide the harvest, considered to be a gourmet treat. Various varieties are available, with either green or purple buds. If you miss the harvesting window then they make a gorgeous cut flower. Traditionally globe artichokes are propagated by division as plants produce offsets; they are grown as short-lived perennials. It is possible to grow globe artichokes from seed, but the results are variable - you may find the flower buds become inedibly spiky.

The cardoon is less well-known, but the same species (*Cynara cardunculus*). It is usually grown as an annual, partly because it is not reliably hardy and partly because it is the stems that are eaten rather than the flower buds. Stems are covered and tied in autumn to blanch them, and then peeled and cooked in soups and stews. It is worth noting that the stems, even on 'spineless' cultivars, can be covered in near invisible spines that are painful if they lodge in the skin - careful handling is required.

The culinary history of the cardoon goes back to ancient Greece and Rome (the plants being native to the Mediterranean), and its use is also common in North Africa. It can also be used as a source of vegetable rennet for cheese-making, but in warmer climates the cardoon has the ability to become invasive.

Jerusalem artichokes

Jerusalem artichokes have a lovely French name - *topinambour*. Elsewhere they are known as sunroots, sunchokes and even earth apples. Native to North America they have no connection to Jerusalem, and are not artichokes - they are *Helianthus tuberosus,* a relative of the sunflower.

In the UK Jerusalem artichokes are a popular crop for allotments, as they make big plants - they can grow up to three metres tall, depending on conditions. And they are an ideal choice for beginners, because they are extremely easy to grow. Tubers are planted like potatoes, although they can be planted earlier in the year because they are far more frost-tolerant. Plants are then left to their own devices all summer, being productive even in fairly poor soils. They are relatively drought-tolerant, although in very dry weather they will eventually die back. They are pest- and disease-free; tubers can be harvested once the tops of the plant have died back in the autumn, but they store well in the ground throughout the winter. Yields can be extremely high, and the tubers can be used like potatoes. They have a slightly nutty flavour, and make a lovely soup.

It sounds too good to be true... and there are a couple of downsides. The first is that any tubers left in the ground will resprout the following year, and it can be difficult to eradicate Jerusalem artichokes from the garden once they have been planted in the soil. It is possible to grow them in containers, although yields will then be smaller - and plants can become top heavy and will need support in windy conditions. But the main problem is that they contain the carbohydrate inulin, which is essentially indigestible. This makes them an ideal food for diabetics and dieters, and means that they act as a prebiotic that is very good at keeping your gut healthy. However, eating Jerusalem artichokes produces a lot of gas - it varies from person to person, but you may find that you are one of the many people for whom eating Jerusalem artichokes is a painful experience.

The method of cooking also affects the resulting ...potency... of the meal, so it may be worth experimenting. Slow cooking, perhaps, or a combination with caraway seeds to ease flatulence. Parboiling the tubers and then discarding the water may also help. But I wouldn't advise serving Jerusalem artichoke surprise to guests!

Jerusalem artichokes are often touted as a good summer screen for an eyesore - and they do grow quite thick quite fast. They don't make a good wind break, however, as the stems get top heavy when they're older and will develop a distinct lean if hit by too much wind. You may, or may not, be lucky enough to see flowers - some varieties flower more than others; varieties are usually selected for the lack of nobbles on their tubers rather than anything else, as they can otherwise be too convoluted to peel.

Chinese artichokes

Chinese artichokes ('crosnes' in French) aren't artichokes either. They're a member of the mint family, *Stachys affinis.* They have another common name, which is jade pearls, which describes quite nicely the tubers - they're small, deeply ringed and iridescent white. It's far more appealing than calling them fat white grubs, but they look like those, too.

Like their mintier relatives, Chinese artichokes are a doddle to grow. Tubers are planted in the spring. Plants reach only around 30 cm tall, but clumps can spread sideways via runners. There is some evidence to suggest that tuber size can be positively affected by giving the plants a rich soil and plenty of water, but tuberisation doesn't begin to occur until autumn when the days are noticeably shorter. Tubers are therefore lifted only once the foliage has completely died back.

Chinese artichokes are easy to grow, but fiddly to clean - the best method is to harvest them directly into a bucket of water and give them a good stir to get rid of any loose dirt before it dries into the crevices. Tubers can be eaten raw or cooked, and are pleasantly crunchy. They make a good substitute for water chestnuts in Chinese meals, but do not store well out of the ground as their thin skin means they rapidly dry out and shrivel.

Propagated via tubers, your Chinese artichoke plants are unlikely to set seed. Like Jerusalem artichokes, however, they are likely to persist in the soil from one year to the next and so will need a permanent bed.

Hamburg parsley

Hamburg parsley (also known as root parsley, among other things) is *Petroselinum crispum* var. *tuberosum,* a proper parsley plant that produces an edible root crop rather than an abundance of leaves. In fact, it may be one of the easiest root crops to grow (I have yet to try it) as, unlike carrots and parsnips it will quite happily cope with a degree of shade. It will grow anywhere you would be able to grow parsley. And it's very hardy, happy outside in all weathers, and can produce a winter supply of parsley leaves for the kitchen even before you get around to harvesting the roots (apparently the parsley flavour is a little more coarse than regular leaf parsley, so use them more sparingly).

Once you have lifted the pale roots you can use them much as you would a carrot - they have a sweetish flavour with a parsley tinge, and make a good addition to roasted roots, or soups and they're not too tough to grate either.

Seeds are available in most seed catalogues here in the UK, although there's not much choice of varieties ('Atika' seems reliable). It's sown in spring, and like parsley I would imagine it can be quite slow to germinate outdoors and it may be worth marking the row with something a bit more eager to get going (radishes are traditional).

Apparently they can be grown in containers, and you can also get away with a second sowing in midsummer that will overwinter and provide roots in early spring - which might be a nice way to extend the season through the 'hungry gap' period. Keep well-watered to avoid roots forking.

Tiger nuts

Tiger nuts are *Cyperus esculentus,* in the same family as papyrus. The edible part is the tubers, pea-sized and produced in profusion from happy plants. And tiger nut plants are relatively easy to keep happy - they enjoy a lot of water and are sometimes grown as marginal plants around the edges of ponds. I would imagine that makes foraging for the tubers a bit tricky, though.

Tiger nuts are popular in Spain, where they are called *chufa* and are ground up and used to produce a drink called horchata. The tubers can also be eaten raw or boiled, and are sweet enough that they were sold in sweet shops in the UK during World War II and the subsequent period of sugar rationing. They fell out of favour once rationing was lifted, though, and tastebuds readjusted to confectionary. These days they are most likely to be found in health food stores or tackle shops - they can be used as carp bait.

If you can source the tubers they are likely to grow, as once dried they keep for years. It's possible that pre-soaking them overnight encourages germination. Tiger nuts can be grown in containers, provided they are kept uniformly wet, which does make harvesting the tubers easier. Plants are frost tender and tubers should be sown after the risk of frost has passed, or indoors. In warmer climates without frost, tiger nuts can become invasive - any tubers left unharvested will regrow the following season.

The tubers are harvested after the tops have died back. Tiger nuts enjoy a good soil, but do not feed them - extra nitrogen causes excessive leafy top growth at the expense of the tubers.

Strawberry spinach

Strawberry spinach, or strawberry blite, has one of the best French names ever - *Epinard fraise,* which makes me think of French private detectives. It's certainly more evocative than *blite,* which doesn't sound nice at all. This is *Chenopodium capitatum,* a North American native and a member of the Chenopod (or Goosefoot family) that is home to more familiar plants such as beetroot and Swiss chard as well as quinoa, tree spinach, Good King Henry and some common weeds.

Strawberry spinach is a dual-purpose plant. It can be grown for its edible leaves, which can be eaten raw (when young) in salads, or cooked like spinach when older. But what distinguishes it from the mass of 'spinach-like' plants is that it grows bright red fruits along the entire length of its stem. They're about the size of a small raspberry, but firmer and a brighter red with black seeds. They are reasonably sweet (more so when fully ripe), with an insipid flavour - although they would brighten up a salad they won't cause much of a stir in the fruit bowl. Having said that, they are abundantly produced and could pack out jams and pies made with tastier fruits. According to Owen Smith, strawberry spinach roots are edible and have a flavor reminiscent of beetroot. If we bug him enough he might write a blog post on the topic in due course.

Strawberry spinach is easy enough to grow, and it's not too hard to source seeds as it is often included in catalogues as an 'oddity'. After you have grown it once you should find it self-seeds, although seedlings are easy to identify and remove if they are growing in the wrong place and as such it is unlikely to become invasive. It would be a simple, if messy, matter to save your own seeds from then on.

For those of you who are interested in alternative uses, the various parts of the plant can be used to produce dyes - explaining one of its common names, which is Indian ink.

The Lost Crops of the Incas

'The Lost Crops of the Incas' is the title of a fascinating book published by The National Academies Press in the USA in 1989. It examines 'little-known plants of the Andes' that the contributors believed held promise for worldwide cultivation. The plants it contains are in no way lost, of course, and are still cultivated in their homeland. It's just that they didn't manage to catch the eye of the Europeans in the same way as tomatoes, potatoes and peppers.

In recent years there has been a surge of interest in these crops, which do indeed hold the promise of providing bountiful harvests in various suitable climate regions across the globe. Many of the ones that are currently most popular are root or tuber crops; they don't suffer from pests and diseases to anything like the extent that the potato does. However, they are not without their problems. As they have not undergone the centuries of selective breeding that have been applied to the potato, they are not well-adapted to life outside the Andean region. Many of them are day-length sensitive, and react badly to being grown in countries where summer days are long; it can be hard to make them crop before midsummer, and to then ripen the crop before the first frosts. But many people are giving them a go, and it's only a matter of time before either the varieties or the growing methods evolve to the point where these plants are productive.

Achocha

Achocha (*Cyclanthera* spp.) hit the heritage seed world a few years ago, and has created quite a wave of interest. Many of its growers find it hard to believe that this plant could be 'lost' at all; others feel that its vigour led to it being lost intentionally!

It is true that achocha is a vigorous, climbing plant. In most of the UK it will grow more successfully outside in the summer than in a greenhouse, where it gets too hot. (Its close relative, the Exploding Cucumber, prefers the indoor environment.)

With its palmate foliage (i.e. the leaves look a bit like an outstretched hand), achocha can sometimes be mistaken for cannabis by the overly suspicious. In fact it is in the Curcurbit family like melons, cucumbers and squash. Unlike its close relatives though, it's not promiscuous and won't cross with your courgettes. It is grown in the same way as beans, with seeds either started indoors in pots or directly outside once the risk of frost has passed. And, like climbing beans, it pays to plant them out in their final position before the tendrils start to tangle. Once they have there is no point patiently unwinding them as they can't coil again - simply cut through them and the plant will grow more.

Achocha tendrils curl delicately around anything in sight. They are a thing of beauty until the point at which they take over the washing line or use the guttering as a bridge into next door's garden. They are often recommended as a good plant to use for a summer screen and given the right conditions can grow for several metres.

While the vines are impressive, the flowers are not. They are tiny, and pale green and you will be hard pressed to spot them. They are, however, a magnet for hoverflies and that usually gives them away. They are rapidly followed by tear-dropped green fruits. Again, they are easy to miss under the foliage. A happy plant is bountiful, so harvest the early fruits young and small while they are tender enough to eat whole. Mature fruits have hard seeds inside that need to be removed before consumption - but it does give you the opportunity to stuff the hollows with something tasty. You can easily save seeds to use in following years - simply scrape them out, dry them off and keep them somewhere dry.

Achocha fruits can be curried, pickled, and used as a pizza topping. People keep coming up with new recipes to cope with the bounty; I discovered that if you grate them you can also feed them to chickens. But the sad truth is that not everyone gets on with their flavour, which is a bit like green pepper without the crunch.

'Achocha' is a Quechua name, and the same plant is known by various other common names including caigua and korila. Although two 'varieties' are commonly available, they are in fact slightly different species. Lady's Slipper is *Cyclanthera pedata* and it grows pairs of fruits that are relatively smooth. Fat Baby is *Cyclanthera brachystachya*, and grows single fruits that look hairy because they are covered in soft, fleshy (and entirely edible) spines. Real Seeds added 'Giant Bolivian Achocha' to their catalogue for 2014 and there may be other variants available in other places.

The Exploding Cucumber is *Cyclanthera explodens* and looks very similar but is considerably more dangerous due to its exploding habit. When the fruits are ripe they spring open and fling seeds out at a surprising rate - eye protection would be advisable to avoid a nasty injury. For obvious reasons, Exploding Cucumber seeds are harder to come by. In fact, ripe achocha fruits do tend to curl once they are cut open, and it's easy to imagine our ancestors selecting the fruits that didn't manage to fling their seeds all over the place, and thus domesticating achocha.

Oca

There are various spellings in use for oca, including oka, and it is also known as the New Zealand Yam. It's no relation to okra, although people will assume that's what you're talking about unless they're in the know. Okra is exotic enough for most kitchen gardeners; oca is still relatively unheard of.

Oca tubers are beautiful things - shiny, rippled to differing extents and available in a rainbow of colours including bright red and orange (variety names tend to be merely a description of the tuber colour). They are grown like potatoes, with tubers planted in spring and pretty much left to their own devices. They benefit from being earthed up, although the tubers don't develop poisonous green patches when exposed to the sun. They are also not affected by blight, not being in the Solanum family - oca is *Oxalis tuberosa*.

The leaves are very clover-like, and although they start off by growing in neat, discrete clumps, by the end of the season they have sprawled considerably. They're edible, and would no doubt add a little zing to a salad, but as they're in the *Oxalis* genus it is probably wise not to eat too many of them in one go - their oxalic acid content can cause problems, less so when cooked.

Stems tend to take on the tinge of the tubers, and in autumn yellow flowers may appear. It's even possible (if you have at least two, compatible, varieties) for them to cross-pollinate and set seed - although it has yet to happen in my garden.

Because oca have not yet adapted to being grown in the UK environment, they don't really start to tuberise until late in the season, and are not harvested until after the first frost has cut down the foliage. Ideally you want a nice long autumn, followed by one short frost and then a couple of weeks of mild weather for the tubers to swell. Although tubers left in the ground can resprout the following year, you can't expect to store your harvest in the soil – they make too tempting a target for slugs and rodents.

Oca is still a new crop, and growing methods are evolving, but it is said that the initial size of the tuber planted has very little effect on the ultimate yield - so eat the larger tubers and keep the smaller ones for replanting. You can chit them like potatoes in early spring (although, again, whether this helps the yield is unknown). They do crop in pots, but are more productive in open ground - although then you have problems with volunteers in future years. They don't harbour diseases in the same way as potatoes, but they can still disrupt your garden plans. The last time I deliberately planted any was 2010, but they still keep coming up!

Some oca tubers can have a very lemony, acid taste. Leaving them in sunlight helps make them sweeter. The general advice is that they can be eaten in the same ways as potatoes, although they have caused mixed reactions in people who have tried to eat them boiled. The best report I have seen was from someone who roasted them, and pronounced them quite lovely prepared that way. Carl Legge also developed a Warm Oca Salad recipe for the Permaculture Magazine website (http://www.permaculture.co.uk/readers-solutions/warm-oca-salad-recipe) and investigations into its culinary potential are still ongoing.

If you decide to grow oca, then I can thoroughly recommend rushing out after rain to take a look - their leaves hold perfect drops of water in a very engaging way. They are most photogenic.

Ulluco

Ulluco (*Ullucus tuberosus)* is another popular unusual tuber - mainly because its egg-shaped tubers come in an even wider range of colours than oca. Sadly it's tricker to grow successfully. In the Basellaceae family, ulluco has an easier time flowering outside of its homeland, but still waits until the last possible minute to begin forming tubers and yields are unsurprisingly low. According to Owen Smith, ulluco plants tend to be riddled with viruses (which could be removed, given an investment in tissue culture) that make them... peaky to say the least. And he also says there is a group of viruses that is common to oca, ulluco and potaotes - so you may not want to give them a space in your garden, no matter how pretty the tubers are.

Unsurprisingly, it's harder to find ulluco tubers to plant than oca tubers, and I am not aware of any particular varieties. If you do decide to grow it then it's useful to know that the leaves are also edible.

Mashua

Another Andean tuber, mashua (also known as añu) is *Tropaeolum tuberosum* - it's a tuber-forming nasturtium. Its foliage is just like that of the nasturtiums we grow for their flowers, and like many of those it has a reasonably ability to climb or at least scramble. I have seen it happily growing in a container inside a greenhouse at Garden Organic Ryton, but tried to grow it myself once with no success.

Mashua is more likely to yield well in the UK than ulluco (at least until new varieties are developed), will flower and produces edible leaves as well. The tubers are supposed to be peppery raw, but milder when cooked. Mashua has its fans, but there are also plenty of people who can't stand it - it seems to be very much an acquired taste. Which would be fine, but considering the lengths you might have to go to in order to find some viable tubers to plant, you may end up feeling disappointed.

Yacón

Yacón is proving a popular choice for many root-crop enthusiasts as, unlike some of the other Andean imports, it is quite easy to grow. All you need is a root crown, or a section of one with a growing tip, and you're on your way. And yacón (*Smallanthus sonchifolius,* syn. *Polymnia edulis)* is a lovely plant - almost cuddly with its large and furry leaves. They almost get large enough to use as fans in the summer, although they're pretty floppy. And it's even possible that your yacón plants (which get quite large, although they don't rival Jerusalem artichokes in a height contest) will flower and produce yellow blooms. But mine tend to produce big, fat flower buds that crumple to mush with the first frost of the autumn. It's very sad.

But the point of yacón is not its furry leaves, or its big, fat flowers. It's the storage tubers it produces underground. You have to be a little careful when you unearth them, as not only can they grow pretty large (think big German sausage) but they are quite brittle and easily snapped. Their crunch is one of their attractive qualities - it means they can be used as a replacement for water chestnuts in Chinese cuisine, and they are much easier to grow.

In fact, yacón tubers don't have much flavour, but they are quite sweet - some people eat them like a fruit. They can also be juiced to produce a syrupy sugar substitute; they are high in fructo-oligosaccharides that act like a prebiotic and encourage the growth of healthy bacteria in the gut, whilst also not jacking up your blood sugar levels or making you fat. On the other hand, some people's digestive systems can be quite sensitive to them and they can make them uncomfortable. Yacón may make you fart, but the effects are reported to be less explosive that those from Jerusalem artichokes.

New varieties of yacón are being developed. A red-skinned variety is available in the UK (from http://www.yakon.co.uk) which is covered by Plant Breeders Rights (which restricts what you can do with it, although growing it for personal consumption is perfectly fine). No doubt there are more varieties floating around, although it's not quite as convenient for dispersal as plants that can be grown from their tubers.

If you do grow yacón and want to carry on growing it then you can lift the roots at the end of the season and keep them frost free until spring (a bit like overwintering dahlias or runner beans) and then plant them out again. They're not too bothered by the cold, and will stay dormant, but I lost mine from the greenhouse in the cold winter of 2010.

Quinoa

Quinoa (*Chenopodium quinoa*) is grown for its grain-like seeds, which are high in high-quality protein and offer a reasonable chance of producing a sizeable 'grain' harvest from a small space in temperate climates. It is often found in health food stores, at least in part because it is gluten-free.

Quinoa is an impressive plant, and shares the Andean signature of being brightly coloured - notable varieties available in the UK include 'Rainbow' - a similar mix of colours to rainbow chard - and the almost fluorescent orange Temuco. You can also eat the leaves as a spinach substitute, as with other Chenopods.

Quinoa seed heads ripen in autumn and are usually ready before the first frosts. However, there is a slight problem with the UK climate in that a damp autumn can cause the seed heads to go mouldy before harvest. Assuming this doesn't happen all you have to do is harvest the ripe seed heads, finish drying them indoors and then thresh the seeds from them - a process that Real Seeds believe is quite easy as long as you're wearing gloves. Threshed seeds are then winnowed to separate them from the chaff. Before you can eat them you need to soak them thoroughly to remove bitter saponins, which are a very good defence against predation by birds.

You can easily save your own seeds for the following year, but be aware that different varieties will cross - so only grow one if you want next year's plants to be the same.

Physalis

There was a time when I was younger when it was all the rage to add exotic fruits to your desserts, and what I came to know as Cape Gooseberries started turning up. They're perfect for upscale dinner parties, as each one comes in its own papery wrapper, which can be left intact or peeled back and used as a handle for dipping the fruit in molten chocolate. They may still be all the rage - I just don't get invited to that kind of party anymore!

Cape gooseberries are *Physalis* fruits, and it seems as though several species are used. I have grown two varieties easily available as seed in the UK - 'Pineapple' and 'Little Lanterns' - both listed as *P. peruviana* with a synonym of *P. edulis.* A quick look at an old Future Foods catalogue suggests other species - *P. angulata* and *P. pruinosa.* Avoid *P. alkekengi,* which is the ornamental Chinese Lanterns and not good to eat.

They also have several common names, including physalis, ground cherries, golden berries, Inca berries and poha. They're grown in a similar way to bush tomatoes, although they are adapted to living in fairly poor soil and so you have to avoid over-feeding them if you want to produce a good crop of fruits rather than a lot of foliage. And they can get quite large... and they do self-seed and so in the right climate they could become a bit of a nuisance. Confining them in containers is one possible way to keep them smaller and encourage them to set and ripen fruits earlier.

The papery cases enclose the fruits throughout their life, which keeps them safe from a lot of pests and other problems, although aphids can still be an issue. And fruits fall to the ground when fully ripe, which makes them easy to spot, but you can also pick them when you're ready and allow them to ripen in the fruit bowl.

When I grew mine we didn't really enjoy them, even dipped into chocolate, but I have since learned that they are nice cooked - and are lovely included in a fruit pie. They have a high pectin content and can also be turned into a good jam. And they do make an impressive show if you invite guests over....

The related tomatillo (*P. ixocarpa)* is not one of the Lost Crops of the Incas as it has its origins in Mexico. It looks very similar to the golden berry, with its fruits covered in papery husks, but is used much more like a tomato. In fact, the tomatillo is the traditional fruit to use in a salsa. The fruits are larger than golden berries, and generally come either in purple or green. In cooler climates they may crop better with some protection, but again they can become large plants when happy. And it appears that pollination is more successful if you have more than one plant.

All of these species are Solanums, related to tomatoes and peppers.

Oriental Vegetables

China and Japan both contain temperate regions, and the vast array of
edible plants from the region is gradually becoming known elsewhere.
Joy Larkcom was one of the key players in making oriental leaves
available in the UK, and her book on the subject is the best that I have
found. It is a very detailed work that includes the many common names
given to each species in different countries and regions - one of the
most confusing aspects of oriental vegetables is trying to pin down what
each one is.

The leafy vegetables remain the most easily accessible and productive,
and many of the brassicas make ideal crops for autumn - sown after
midsummer they have less of a tendency to bolt and can crop into the
winter if given some protection.

While seed catalogues are catching up and offering an increasing range
of oriental vegetables, mainly aimed at salad and stir-fry leaves, I
suspect they are only really the tip of the iceberg. But here are some of
the most easily sourced and grown, not to mention tasty, ones to try.

Mizuna

Mizuna is a lovely leafy green with strappy, serrated leaves. It's a variety
of *Brassica rapa,* grows in fairly sedate clumps and is reasonably cold
tolerant. It can be eaten raw, or cooked into stir-fries. Leaves have a
mild mustard flavour.

Mizuna has a tendency to bolt; sowing later in the year and keeping
plants well-watered will help to suppress that, as will regular harvesting
of the leaves. When it does flower, the bright yellow flowers are very
pretty and edible - you can use the flowering shoots of all the oriental
brassicas as a kind of broccoli substitute.

Mibuna

Mibuna is a similar plant, another *B. rapa,* with unserrated strappy
leaves and a stronger flavour than mizuna. They're both good in

containers if kept well-watered and a good place to start if you're looking for an easy introduction to oriental greens.

Kailaan

The problem with traditional British brassicas (Brussels sprouts, kale, cabbages and sprouting broccoli) is two-fold: they are large plants and they are in the ground for a long time. They are therefore not very suitable for cultivation in containers and small gardens. A possible solution is to replace them with oriental brassicas, which are generally smaller plants and produce a harvest more quickly. Kailaan is Chinese broccoli (also sometimes known as Chinese kale), a variety of *B. oleracea.* They are very quick - you can pick whole plants young, from just 20-30 days after sowing, or wait until they are larger and cut them up to three times. Even if they bolt and start to flower, the whole plant is edible.

You can get a similar crop from Rapini (also known as Cima di rapa and broccoli raab), which are turnip greens, but they don't count as an oriental vegetable and are more commonly eaten in Mediterranean countries.

Radishes

Firm favourites in Asia, daikon and mooli are radishes (*Raphanus sativus)* although they put our little salad radishes to shame - these are big roots and can end up even larger than big carrots. They're more like the winter radishes that are grown for storage, although there are varieties that are sown in spring for a summer harvest. The roots are eaten raw and grated into salads, or sliced and cooked in stir fries or added to any number of pickles.

The earthy heat of radishes isn't to everyone's taste, and you may not have a garden suitable for giant root crops. Another possibility is to grow regular salad radishes (generally recommended for new or junior gardeners because of their sheer speed) and to let them go to seed. They bolt very easily, and at that point you wouldn't want to eat the woody roots - but you can eat the crunchy seed pods instead. They make a peppery addition to salads and stir-fries when eaten young and fresh. Don't let them get too old or the seeds will start to mature and the pods won't be as nice.

There is a variety of radish grown specifically for its pods - the Rat's Tail radish, commonly found in heritage seed catalogues. It runs to seed very quickly, to provide an abundant pod harvest. But the seed pods of all radishes are edible; some are hotter than others, so try a few and see which ones you prefer.

Pak choi

Pak choi is another brassica - *B. rapa* var. *chinensis* - and a lovely leafy vegetable. It makes discrete plants, although height is determined by variety. Some are bred to be grown as baby vegetables, harvested whole for salad leaves when very young. Others are more statuesque, quite similar to chard in their appearance with glossy green (spoon-shaped) leaves and white stems. They can be sown right through the growing season, and again if they decide to bolt it's not a disaster. In fact, they are often sold in China just at the flowering stage. And there's a lovely new red-tinged version available, if you don't mind F1 seeds.

Pak choi can be a bit of a challenge (although I suspect that choosing the right variety for your location is half the battle), and you may find tatsoi (*Brassica rapa* var. *rosularis)* a little easier. It grows low in tidy clumps, with little leaves that are almost pear-shaped. It's very hardy and crops through the winter if given some protection; harvesting enough leaves for dinner is a time-consuming occupation, but it's a very easy plant to grow.

There are far more oriental brassicas than I could touch on here (I haven't even mentioned the mustard leaves) and if you like interesting salads or stir-fries then it's an area that warrants further investigation and experimentation. There are also oriental greens from other plant families.

Chrysanthemum greens

The garland chrysanthemum, *Glebionis coronaria,* is also called chop suey greens. It has a distinctive and unusual flavour, which may explain why it has been slower to catch on in Western cultures than the more familiar brassicas. Although widely adopted, and popular, as a food plant across Asia, the garland chrysanthemum has its origins in the Mediterranean.

Quick growers, Chrysanthemum greens can be used as a catch crop. If you want a fairly continuous supply you will need to sow two or three times in a year, although if you have a suitable climate it can be encouraged to self-seed. The leaves and stems are the main parts eaten, but the flowers are also used and can be made into tea.

Plants prefer cooler weather and you may struggle with them in a hot summer. They grow more lushly if given a fertile soil and kept well-watered. They are often grown entirely as ornamental plants, so this is one edimental that would feel at home in the flower bed. It's worth letting a few flower – they're not only pretty, but they attract beneficial insects as well.

Chinese chives

Chinese chives are garlic chives, *Allium tuberosum,* and they are grown very much in the same way as regular chives. They are perennial plants, and tend to get relegated to the herb bed - but in China and Japan they are elevated to the much more useful position of vegetable.

Garlic chives have slightly flatter, strappier leaves than regular chives. They don't have the pretty purple flowers; instead they have more delicate, white star-shaped flowers that are very beautiful. The flowers can be eaten along with the leaves and stems, and the whole plant has a mild garlic flavour - they are to garlic what chives are to onions.

But if you grow enough of them, you can blanch them - the bleached stems are very much a delicacy in the Far East. To blanch plants, cut to the ground and then cover with a light-excluding bucket or forcing jar for three to four weeks. Blanching weakens the plant, so it's best to have several specimens and only blanch each one once a year.

Plants are easily grown from seed, although initial growth can be slow and seed doesn't stay viable for more than a year so make sure yours is fresh. In theory plants could self-seed, although mine hasn't done and I will have to divide it to increase my stock.

With a bit of protection garlic chives can crop through the winter. I have never seen any varieties, but apparently in China they have selected varieties specifically for leaf production, or for flower production.

According to Chiltern Seeds, garlic chive flowers smell like old-fashioned roses and pots on the windowsill can scent the whole room. I have never noticed, but will have a good sniff next time they start to flower. This is after I have divided my plant in the hope of having enough to try blanching them, eating the flowers and adding the leaves to absolutely everything!

Peashoots

The humble pea may seem like a mainstream ingredient, but if you ever see pea shoots on sale they are extremely expensive - because they don't lend themselves to commercial production, deteriorate rapidly, and are too fragile for extensive freighting. In short, they are a perfect candidate for the home gardener with a taste for the good things in life.

Pea shoots are the leafy tips of pea plants, generally produced specifically by sprouting seeds closely together and harvesting the tops two or three times while the plant is young, then composting the lot and starting a new batch. They can also be nipped off the plants you're growing for their pea pods, although taking too many might reduce the yields.

Delicate, frondy things with a mild pea flavour, they make a lovely garnish or salad ingredient and can liven up winter sandwiches - grown indoors they are a year-round crop.

You have to be careful when choosing seeds for sprouting, as many seeds are treated with chemicals before they are packed. That normally means buying seeds grown organically for sprouting, and a trip to the local health food shop. But peas are obliging and you can soak and sprout dried green peas sold for eating. In fact, that's one of the cheapest ways of getting your hands on pea seeds in volume, and the variety doesn't matter very much when the plants aren't allowed to mature.

If you do use a horticultural variety of pea then it pays to be a bit choosy - hardier round-seeded varieties might be better in winter; maincrop wrinkled-seeded varieties the rest of the time. My favourite so far is Douce Provence, a heritage dwarf variety that doesn't tangle up too badly; some peas rapidly produce tendrils and a thicket that Prince Charming would struggle to hack his way through.

Peashoots are usually harvested by snipping them off with scissors. Providing you don't cut below the bottom leaves they will carry on growing for another harvest or two before they are exhausted and need replacing. I do know someone who pulls them up and eats the whole thing - roots and all, but he grows his in vermiculite so at least they don't have compost clinging to them.

Soy beans

Soy beans (*Glycine max*) have to be one of the most common crops in the world. They are widely eaten as fresh beans and dried beans, and processed into many products including soy oil, tofu and soy milk, soy sauce and miso and even soy flour. And there are varieties used for animal feed as well.

But for all its agricultural popularity, soy beans can be a difficult plant to grow for a gardener, as they are particularly dependent on both day length and temperature to trigger the different stages of growth. New varieties are being developed that are suitable for different geographical locations. A few years ago I tried, unsuccessfully, to grow 'Ustie' here in the UK - I failed even to get the seeds to germinate. The current variety on offer to the British public seems to be 'Elena'. In countries where soy beans thrive there are numerous varieties - green-seeded for edamame, black-seeded for drying, and yellow-seeded for processing - but that seems a long way off in cooler climates.

If you do manage to find a suitable variety, and get the seeds to germinate (they are prone to rotting in cold soil, so do not over-water before they begin to grow) then you can treat soy beans like other climbing beans - as tender annuals - although they require a longer season to crop well. They are self-pollinating, and if you want fresh beans (i.e. edamame) then you pick the pods once the beans inside have swelled, but whilst the pods themselves are still fresh and green. If you're aiming for dried beans then most likely you will have to pull up the whole plants at the end of the season and hang them upside down indoors to finish drying.

Another issue with beans and other legumes is that, whilst often touted as 'nitrogen fixing' they do this in symbiosis with suitable strains of soil bacteria (rhizobia). If you're growing runner beans and peas on an allotment then the relevant rhizobia will have long since colonised the soil, but if you're growing something more unusual (or in sterilised potting compost) then they won't be present and crop growth can be underwhelming as a result. The quick solution is to inoculate the seeds with the right bacteria at sowing time, and in the US it is possible to buy various strains of rhizobia, although the UK gardening market is slow to catch on. It looks as though the most suitable strain for soy beans (and the mung beans I am about to mention) is *Bradyrhizobium japonicum,* but I am by no means an expert and in fact it seems that the science around these symbiotic relationships is still very much being uncovered.

The slightly slower solution is to persevere; although the rhizobia you need may not have been present in sufficient numbers during the first growing season, they seem to magically accumulate once suitable host plants are being grown. Crops should therefore be heartier in the following seasons (providing you are growing in the soil, and not sterile potting compost each year). At the end of the growing season you can tell whether your plants have been able to form a symbiotic relationship by checking for little nodules on the roots. If they are present then leaving the roots in the soil, or moving them to the compost heap, will mean their continuing presence for future years.

Mung beans

Mung beans (*Vigna radiata,* formerly *Phaseolus aureus)* are very small, usually green beans. Although they are used in oriental cooking as beans, they are most familiar to Western gardeners as the source of bean sprouts. Soak them overnight, drain and then rinse twice a day and they will rapidly morph into crunchy bean sprouts (although they are never as straight as the ones you buy); they need to be kept in the dark to have the traditional, blanched white stems and mild flavour. A spoonful of seeds becomes a jarful of sprouts that can be eaten raw in salads or lightly cooked for stir-fries. The key to the whole process is hygiene; discard any batches that start to look or smell mouldy, and any seeds that fail to sprout. Sprouts are touted as a way to while away the winter months and have fresh veggies during the 'hungry gap', but they are temperature dependent and the chilly nature of my current kitchen isn't conducive to their culture in cold weather.

It is possible to grow your mung beans through to maturity. Again, they are tender, climbing plants that need a long season to mature into dried beans. You can harvest young pods, very early before the beans are prominent, and eat them like mangetout. If you wish to harvest dried beans then you will likely have to bring the plants indoors at the end of the season to finish drying. Beans are dry enough for storage when they shatter when hit with a hammer; if they are not fully dried they will rot. Once they are fully dried a short stint in the freezer kills off any insect pests that remain, if this is an issue in your location.

And again, these beans will struggle to find their perfect symbiosis partner in your garden to begin with. So be prepared for your first attempt at growing them to be a little lacklustre, and try again the following year.

Perennial Pleasures

A traditional kitchen garden is dominated by annual vegetables (or biennial and perennial plants grown as annuals). It has its yearly cycles of soil preparation, sowing and planting, harvesting and composting and crop rotation. There are peaks and troughs of effort, with spring sowing being a particularly hectic time.

Permaculture tends towards a different approach, adding far more edible and useful perennial plants to the garden. The idea is partly to minimise the effort and inputs to the garden, as once planted perennials require less maintenance than annual plants - often at different times of the year. And perennials often crop early, or late, in the season and provide food when there is little else around.

A kitchen garden based on perennials (especially when carefully structured into a forest garden that mirrors the many ecological niches of a natural woodland) can be very productive with far less human intervention - but it does involve growing and eating different things, or having an 'annual' patch elsewhere for staple crops.

There are a few common perennial crops - rhubarb, asparagus and globe artichokes - but once you move beyond that you're into a whole new world of interesting fruits and vegetables that rarely, if ever, make it onto supermarket shelves.

Japanese wineberry

A lot of soft fruit is perennial, and bushes tend to be easily managed. Each has its own routine of pruning, and most require a feed of compost or well-rotted manure in the spring time, but then it's just a matter of keeping an eye out for pests, watering in very dry weather and collecting the crop when it's ripe.

The Japanese wineberry (*Rubus phoenicolasius*) makes a lovely addition to the fruit garden or a perennial patch. It's grown in much the same way as raspberries and blackberries, but has striking red stems covered in prickles rather than thorns. Beautiful white flowers develop into fruits encased in their calyces until they're completely ripe - keeping them safe from almost all pests, including the birds. And the ripe red fruit (produced in August) have a lovely flavour and rarely make it back to the kitchen. A mature bush can produce stems a couple of metres tall, but is easily trained across a wall or wires.

Canes that have fruited are pruned out, and the new growth tied in. Once you have one plant it is easily propagated as the tips layer - peg them down into the soil to encourage them to root and sever them from the parent plant once they have. It's also possible to propagate from hardwood cuttings.

Hablitzia

Hablitzia tamnoides is a permaculture poster child - a plant so uncommon that it doesn't have a common name in English. Stephen Barstow calls it Caucasian spinach, as this climbing leafy green has its origins in the Caucasus. It is very hardy, surviving the worst of northern European winters and springing into life well before most other leafy greens in a cold climate. The young shoots and leaves are eaten like spinach.

Hablitzia can climb to three metres and is at home in shady conditions, given its native tendency to grow in woodlands. A perennial, it tends to grow slowly in its first year (if grown from seed) and then grow more vigorously in subsequent seasons. (The general rule for perennials is that in the first year they 'sleep', in the second they 'creep' and in the third year they 'leap' - unlike annuals and biennials they spend the first season or two settling in, and then just go nuts.)

There is a resurgence of interest in Hablitzia, particularly in Nordic countries and it is easiest to source seeds and plants there. However, it is spreading slowly in suitable climate regions (ones with cool, wet starts to the year) and as it is fairly drought-tolerant outside of its main growing season and unfussy as to soil, Hablitzia could well become a mainstay of the 'hungry gap' perennial garden in future years. If you do manage to get your hands on some seeds, it seems that cold stratification is the key to germination - winter sowing outdoors may well be more successful than indoor sowing, as the seeds don't seem to like germinating when temperatures are too high.

Good King Henry

Hablitzia is the only species in its genus, but it's in the same family (the Chenopodiaceae, or Goosefoot) as plenty of other familiar and unfamiliar vegetables. Another commonly grown perennial vegetable in the same family is Good King Henry - *Chenopodium bonus-henricus.* Good King Henry is often sold as a herb and placed in the herb garden, but it is eaten (where it is eaten) as a leafy green vegetable. The leaves themselves are no great shakes - they're green and abundantly produced, but a little mealy and probably best eaten cooked. And this is another plant that contains oxalic acid and is therefore best consumed in moderation. But the key to enjoying Good King Henry seems to lie in eating the flowering shoots. Again, these are freely produced on a mature plant, quite early in the spring, and are lightly cooked and eaten like asparagus. You can also blanch the shoots if you want an extra-special treat, but as usual the plant will need plenty of time to recover once you have.

If you eat the flowering shoots then you won't have any problems with your Good King Henry self-seeding, which is potentially an issue although unwanted seedlings are easily identified and removed. In fact, the plant I have had in my garden for several years is now mature and productive but I have seen very few seedlings from it.

Daubenton Kale

Perennial kales are another permaculture favourite, as they provide much-needed leafy goodness throughout the bitterest of winter weathers. The advantage of perennial kales is that the plants do not have to be replaced every year, but the disadvantage of perennial kales is that they are still subject to the same pests and diseases as annual brassicas - particularly, in my experience, whitefly.

Although there are unnamed varieties of perennial kale, Daubenton kale is reputed to have the best flavour. It is also said not to flower and set seed, and so has to be propagated vegetatively and can be hard to come by. However, the Heritage Seed Library catalogue for 2012 included a listing for Daubenton Kale seeds - so it seems they are sometimes produced and available.

Another perennial brassica that is far easier to find is 9-star broccoli, a kind of halfway house between purple sprouting broccoli and cauliflowers, although it is a short-lived perennial past its best after a few years. Opinion is divided as to whether it's worth growing or simply a pest magnet and a poor substitute for annual purple sprouting broccoli (or even white sprouting broccoli), which is a gourmet treat well worth growing if you can afford the space it takes up for most of the year.

Sea Kale

Kale and broccoli are easy enough to buy, but unless you live by the seaside then savouring their cousin sea kale (*Crambe maritima*) is a more difficult prospect unless you grow your own. Sea kale is another perennial vegetable available early in the year, the more so because it is forced (like rhubarb) so that it produces tender white leaves, shoots and flower heads. They were popular with the Victorians, but have fallen out of favour since then and no doubt qualify as a forgotten vegetable.

Sea kale is often sold as 'thongs' that are planted in spring. It can also be grown from seed, but that adds a year on to the time before the first harvest - the plant has to be strong enough before it can be forced, and so this is not done before its third season. If you have once of those nice Victorian forcing pots (or, alternatively a dark bucket) then you can force it *in situ* by clearing away any debris, piling dry leaves over the crown and then excluding light with your bucket. Shoots are ready around 3 months later, and plants should be uncovered to recover from May onwards.

You can also dig up crowns after the first frosts of winter and bring them inside to force, so you can have crops through the winter. But after abuse of this kind the crowns will almost certainly be exhausted and need to be replaced.

Clumps can be propagated by division, or by taking your own root cuttings, so once you've developed a taste for sea kale it's an easy plant to keep in stock.

Perennial alliums

The allium family is bursting with edible, perennial members. Egyptian walking onions are an example of tree onions (*Allium × proliferum*), onions that grow in clumps and develop aerial bulbils (little bulbs) at the top of stalks. Late in the season, when the plant starts to sag, these bulblets are 'planted' in the ground by their parent and so the clump 'walks', gradually expanding in all favourable directions. The result is a clump of perennial onions, all parts of which are edible. The green leaves (like giant chives or spring onions) are available almost year-round, and the bulblets themselves are edible although they are quite fiddly to peel. And you can dig up the clump, eat some of the subterranean bulbs and replant the rest.

As well as the walking onions, the Welsh onion (*A. fistulosum*) is reasonably common - you can find seeds in the herb section of most catalogues - and comes in two varieties. One has white stems and one has red, although the leaves are green in both cases. Care and harvest is the same as for tree onions, but the Welsh onion produces rather stunning white flower heads in early summer that are a magnet for bees. While they're in flower you can't harvest them - more because of the danger of being stung rather than any great difference in the leaves. They do die back in the worst of the winter weather, but rapidly return with fresh leaves.

In a similar vein, Babington's leek (*A. ampeloprasum babingtonii*) is a perennial leek, producing edible leaves and shoots early in the spring. Again, you can eat the underground bulbs, and the aerial bulbils, and even the flowers are edible.

Potato onions (*A. cepa aggregatum*) are a perennial version of the common onion (*A. cepa*). Each planted bulb divides into 5-15 new bulbs over the season, in a similar manner to shallots. These are then lifted and the largest can be stored for replanting in spring. If a potato onion is too small in its first season it may just grow into a larger, undivided bulb - it should divide as normal if replanted the following year. Seed is rarely produced by potato onions and so they have to be propagated via the bulbs.

These are just a few of the more common perennial alliums available, and none of them should be too hard to track down. There are plenty of others, and it's perfectly possible to develop an allium obsession, but some can be invasive in certain climates and it's worth checking that you can keep new varieties under control before you introduce them to your garden. And they're all susceptible to the same pests and diseases, which can make it tricky to eradicate something like leek rust if it finds a home in your garden.

Medlars

Most of the plants mentioned in this book are relatively small and would be able to find a home even in a small garden, but the medlar (*Mespilus germanica*) is a tree and can grow to 6 metres in time. It was once a popular fruit, but has fallen by the wayside because it is steadfastly unsuited to commercial production and distribution.

The medlar apparently has an unattractive French name (*'cul de chien'*) because the fruit has an unusual shape. It's a bit like a round, brown apple, but it has a bottom that is folded in on itself and has a papery edge, rather like it's wearing a paper hat from a Christmas cracker. The fruits ripen in October, and are left on the tree to soften and 'blet' -

essentially start to rot. Even once they are harvested they are left to continue bletting until the flesh is so soft it can be eaten with a spoon. It has a flavour akin to spiced apple that you're unlikely to experience unless you have your own tree. And if you can find the space they are rather stunning specimens, as the fruits are preceded by large white flowers in May.

I have never yet heard of anyone with a glut of medlars, but should you tire of eating them with a spoon then they are nice in pies and make good preserves as well.

Mulberries

The mulberry is another tree fruit that was once popular but defies the might of commercialisation. Unlike the medlar, however, it is not because the fruit is too hard to eat without lengthy storage - in fact, it's just the opposite. Mulberries are so soft and squidgy they are almost impossible to harvest without covering yourself in their juice, and would disintegrate long before they made it to supermarket shelves. And so mulberries are a delicacy rarely experienced except by home growers.

The mulberry you want is *Morus nigra,* and the trees can grow to 10 metres although they're relatively slow growing and it should be possible to keep one smaller in a container if necessary (they have a natural tendency towards a bushy habit). The fruits have to be eaten fresh as they rot rapidly, and as they fall to the ground when fully ripe this can involve a bit of scrabbling around. You could try spreading a sheet of some sort underneath the tree to keep the ripe fruit out of the dirt; the fruits ripen around midsummer.

As a slow-grower, planting a young mulberry is an investment in your future - once it has settled in it should outlive you and provide good crops for several decades. They require little care beyond a good feed of compost in the spring and a little pruning (while dormant) to remove any damaged branches or those that are growing in inconvenient directions.

Goji berries

Goji berries were all the rage a couple of years ago as they were promoted as the latest 'superfruit' - packed to the brim with healthy antioxidants that make up for these damaging modern lives we all lead. The truth is that there are plenty of 'superfoods' that are less exotic - broccoli and blackberries and blackcurrants being common and popular crops that pack a nutritional punch. But if you have developed a taste for goji berries then it's certainly easy enough to grow your own and they are robust perennial plants.

The first step is to source your plants or seeds from a reputable supplier - the goji berry (*Lycium barbarum)* is a member of the Solanaceae family (along with tomatoes, peppers and aubergines) and as such could in theory carry diseases that would migrate into these other crops. But the goji is increasingly available in mainstream plant catalogues, so this is not too much of an issue.

Goji plants like full sun - I know this because I had a trio, planted in a line. Two were productive, the third was overshadowed and was not. It's not dead, it's just not fruitful. And they are not a good choice for a small garden as they grow arching stems up to 2.5 metres long that are spiny - not unduly so, but enough to give you a good scratch if they're planted by a path. They would make a good addition to a boundary hedge, as a fruitful deterrent to unauthorised entry as well as protecting wildlife from neighbourhood cats.

They can be grown in largish containers, but are happiest in the ground. When young they can be susceptible to drought, so keep them well-watered until they have established - at which point they become virtually unkillable (they are very hardy).

Gojis seem to produce fruit on stems that are at least a year old, so you have to take that into account when you are pruning back their exuberance. The fruits are small (perhaps the size of raisins) and ripen from green to bright red - fruiting stems look very much like strings of holiday lights. They don't all ripen at once, it's a bit like tomatoes ripening in sequence on the vine. Unless they are to be used fresh, fruits are usually dried for storage, although I would imagine they also freeze reasonably well.

The fruits are seedy and it would be easy enough to save your own seed, but plants can also be propagated from cuttings and from layers (which I have not seen advised elsewhere, but it worked for me).

Goji berries are not a new introduction to the UK and can be found growing wild in some places. They used to be called 'The Duke Of Argyll's Tea' as the leaves can be used as a tea substitute - but given that this is a solanum you'd be well-advised to ensure you have correctly identified the plant before you brew up a pot.

Unusual Herbs

A 'cottage garden' has become a garden design choice, with an informal design, traditional materials and a mixture of ornamental and edible planting. But the original cottage gardens were far more useful, and would have been patches filled with edible plants and medicinal herbs, with the odd ornamental plant filling in the gaps and feeding the bees. A lot of traditional herb lore has fallen by the wayside, but the tide is turning and people are once again starting to grow medicinal herbs, or dye plants, kitchen herbs and even brewing and strewing herbs. There are plenty of less common herbs to choose, even if you stick to the edible ones; some have fascinating histories and others have exotic origins.

Costmary

Costmary (*Tanacetum balsamita* or *Chrysanthemum balsamita)* was originally a meadow plant, and is also known as Alecost because it was used to flavour beer before hops (*Humulus lupulus)* took over. Its fragrant leaves repel silverfish, and so were used as bookmarks (particularly in bibles) to protect the paper from being eaten. The leaves can be used in pot pourris, but are also used for herbal teas and young leaves can be chopped into salads in spring.

Costmary is an unfussy herb, putting up with partial shade and poor soil and hardy enough to withstand cold weather and put on new growth in early spring. But its spreading rhizomes can create a dense mat that will spread over time, so it could become invasive under the right conditions.

Plants grow to around a metre high when in flower, and are more likely to flower in a sunny spot - leaves are harvested before flowering, and used fresh or dried for storage. The plants spread around 45 cm. The silvery foliage, daisy-like flowers and fragrance make this an attractive choice for the garden, and according to Jekka McVicar fresh leaves can be used to relieve the pain of bites and stings.

Sorrel

There are many different sorrel (*Rumex* spp.) species, and the thing that they have in common is a strong, acidic and lemony flavour. The first sorrel I added to our garden was a broad-leaved sorrel (*Rumex acetosa 'Shchavel')* from the Heritage Seed Library. It is a hardy perennial, and one of the first leafy greens to emerge in the garden in spring. It's incredibly low maintenance, and the chickens went nuts for it. Unfortunately its lemony flavour wasn't as big a hit with the human members of the household, as even small amounts in a mixed salad make you feel as though you've been hit in the face with a lemon. We have not yet been brave enough to try the excellent soup this species is supposed to make.

The gourmet choice for sorrel is *Rumex scutatus,* the Buckler Leaf (or French) sorrel. While the broad-leaved sorrel makes a tall plant that can reach 60 cm or more when it flowers, the Buckler Leaf sorrel is more of a low-growing creeper. The shield-shaped leaves are much smaller, and harvesting enough for a salad is a slower job. If it's happy, the plant will spread into a sprawling clump, so you'll rapidly have a plentiful supply if you like it. It's easy enough to keep under control if you prefer it in small amounts.

The edimental choice is red- or blood-veined sorrel, *Rumex sanguineus* var. *sanguines.* It's a larger plant, similar in size and leaf-shape to broad-leaved sorrel, but with the glorious red leaf veins normally associated with ruby chard. I found it to be slower-growing in my garden than the plain green varieties, but it is fully hardy. Leaves are apparently nice in salads when picked young, in spring. As they get older they can get a bit tough. I wouldn't know, as I have yet to find an efficient way of protecting my sorrel plants from the attentions of house sparrows, who find it as delicious as the chickens do. They also eat their way through any plantings of leaf beet and chard, a habit they have only developed in the last couple of years. I didn't know sparrows ate greens, and before I caught them in the act I assumed the missing chunks had been eaten by slugs and snails.

The lemony flavour in sorrels comes from oxalic acid, and so the leaves should be consumed in moderation although cooking does reduce the oxalic content somewhat. According to the PFAF database, the juice from the leaves of broad-leaved sorrel can be used for curdling milk.

(The Caribbean drink 'sorrel' is made from the red sepals of *Hibiscus sabdariffa,* a tender sun-loving member of the Malvaceae family that's also known as Roselle.)

Lemon balm

Lemon is quite a common flavour amongst herbs (as well as sorrel there's lemongrass, lemon verbena, lemon thyme, lemon-scented geraniums and even lemon catnip), but lemon balm is quite different to sorrel and has become one of my favourite herbs.

Lemon balm is related to mint, and so is as easy as garden mint to grow (which does mean that in some places it could become invasive). I allow it to self-seed in the garden, as it's endlessly useful and easy enough to root out if it's growing somewhere I don't want it to.

Mints and lemon balm are all happy enough in containers for short periods of time, providing they get enough water. They need dividing in spring, or repotting into a larger pot, as they get unhappy when their roots are constricted. And they do not play well with others; their roots will crowd out anything less robust, and the flavours of different mints are thought to mingle if they are grown together.

The good news is that, if allowed to flower, they are all excellent for attracting and feeding beneficial insects - including bees.

A fully hardy perennial, lemon balm can grow to around 75 cm tall, but regular clipping helps to encourage a continuous supply of fresh leaves. There are two versions, the plain species (*Melissa officinalis*) and the variegated *M. officinalis 'Aurea',* which is slightly less tolerant of too much sun.

Lemon balm leaves make a lovely tea which is refreshing and (allegedly) good for your memory as well as your digestion. It's also anti-bacterial and anti-viral, so it's a great one to have on hand in case you feel like you're coming down with a bug. Leaves can be added to fruit salads and used to flavour syrups, or added to salads and stuffings. I have a lovely recipe for potato salad that simply involves cooked potatoes, mayonnaise and chopped mint leaves; I will have to try replacing the mint with lemon balm, I suspect it would be lovely.

Stevia

Stevia (*Stevia rebaudiana),* also known as the Aztec herb and sweet leaf, is a tender perennial native to the Americas. It has a long history of use as a sweetener in various cultures, as its leaves are very sweet. They can be used fresh, or dried, in cooking or herbal teas.

The plants can grow to around 60 cm tall, and in my experience can get quite leggy. They have to be brought indoors for the winter to protect them from the cold, and Jekka McVicar's advice is that they should be cut back quite low at this point to re-sprout in spring. My first plant died over the winter, I think from lack of water while I was otherwise occupied with people rebuilding my house; I am trying again this year.

Stevia is a new arrival on UK shores, as it has only recently been granted a license to be grown and used in the European Union. Previously, here as in the US, stevia was deemed to be a potentially harmful food additive, despite many years of apparently safe use in other countries. There may have been some politics involved, but the good news (for Brits at least) is that it is now possible to buy both plants and seeds of stevia here, and the plant is easy to grow (although perhaps easier treated as an annual).

Jekka McVicar suggests that germination can be erratic, and stocks are best increased by taking cuttings in early summer. She is one of the few people I know of who are using stevia, and she includes several recipes in 'Jekka's Herb Cookbook'. It was whilst listening to Jekka on Woman's

Hour one morning that I realised I had never sampled my stevia. For some reason I didn't find it enticing, this leafy herb that doesn't look as though it belongs in a sugar bowl. But I had a little nibble, and by jove it's as sweet as they say it is.

Although its low-calorie sweetness is amazing and very useful, stevia doesn't entirely replace sugar. It can withstand high temperatures, so cooking with it is not a problem, but it doesn't caramelise or feed yeasts and so its contribution to home-baking is limited. The sweetness of the leaves will also vary according to the exact conditions in which the plant is grown and the time of year and the age of the leaves, and so it is far from the standardised sweeteners we are used to.

Perilla

Perilla, or shiso, is *Perilla frutescens* and a popular herb in Japan. With its large, crinkled leaves (in green or stunning red/ purple) it makes a lovely edimental addition to the herb garden. An annual plant, growing to around 90 cm tall, perilla is only half hardy, likes a sunny spot and is a member of the Lamiaceae family.

Young leaves and thinned seedlings (or sprouts) can be eaten raw, in sandwiches and salads. Older leaves are used as a garnish or flavouring or cooked in stir-fries. The flavour is spicy, often described as a cross between cumin and coriander. The purple version is used as a food dye, and lends its colour to pickles and Umeboshi (pickled ume, *Prunus mume* fruits) in particular.

If your growing season is long enough, your perilla may flower and set seed before the first frosts and the seeds are also used in pickles or toasted and salted as a snack. Of course, you could simply save your own seeds for sowing next year, or sprouting through the winter. And if frost threatens, the flowers themselves are edible.

During the growing season, harvest the growing tips first as these not only have the most concentrated flavour, but removing them encourages the plant to be bushier and more productive. There is some suggestion that perilla is poisonous to horses and cattle, though, so be careful where you allow it to grow (and possibly self-seed) if you share your environment with animals.

Paracress

Paracress is an interesting plant, known variously as the toothache plant, Szechuan buttons and electric buttons, the Peek-a-boo plant or the eyeball plant. Scientifically it has a slightly less exciting name, *Acmella oleracea* (previously *Spilanthes oleracea or S. acmella).*

The 'toothache' aspect comes from its ability to (temporarily) cause numbness in the mouth. Before the numbness, however, there is a distinctly odd fizzing sensation - which is what gives rise to the name 'electric buttons'. I first tried it on an unsuspecting Dave Hamilton (author of 'Grow Your Food For Free') when he came for a visit. As he regularly leads foraging walks, I guessed Dave would be game for sampling an odd plant in my garden. He was more game than I was, taking a big chomp out of the flower I handed him, while I took a more ladylike nibble out of mine. The result, for me, was a mild fizzing and subsequent numbness. Dave found the stronger symptoms rather disconcerting, and as it promotes the production of saliva, ended up doing quite a lot of spitting in the garden.

As well as their unusual effects (and paracress has been used, apparently, in some concoctions by bleeding-edge chef Heston Blumenthal), paracress flowers look very odd. The leaves are low-growing and dark green, and the flowers float above them on sturdy stems. They are fat round things, with the look and feel of the centre of daisies, yellow for most of their length and then red right at the top. Hence the references to eyeballs in some of their common names - I think of them as alien eyeballs, as they are most often yellow, with red 'pupils'.

I have yet to try them, but the leaves are also edible and can be added shredded (in small amounts) into salads. Once cooked they lose their unusual qualities somewhat but are used as a flavouring in their native Brazil.

Paracress is a tender perennial; I am attempting to over-winter some in my greenhouse to see how hardy they are, but they're easily grown from seed as an annual in cool climates. Whether you'll find a use for them beyond botanical 'pop rocks' is another matter.

Vietnamese coriander

Vietnamese coriander (*Persicaria odorata)* is also known as Vietnamese mint or hot mint. It is related to neither mint nor coriander, being a member of the Polygonaceae family. As its name suggests, it is commonly used in Vietnamese cooking and has been one of the popular new introductions to the UK herb scene in the past couple of years.

Vietnamese coriander is a tender perennial. If grown outdoors in the UK it has to be treated as an annual, although it can also be grown indoors as a houseplant as long as you don't put it on your sunniest windowsill - it can scorch in strong sunlight. In warmer climates it is a rampant grower that will romp away and could easily become invasive.

The leaves are mainly green, but have a characteristic maroon 'V' shape pointing away from the stem. Flowers are unlikely, even indoors, outside of the tropics but would be small and white in late summer. The flavour is strongly pungent, with a hint of lime, and the leaves are always used raw, added as a condiment at the end of cooking, or added to salads. Leaves toughen as they age, so harvest the young leaves in preference.

I haven't seen seeds for sale, but once you have a plant it is easily propagated from cuttings, which may even root in a glass of water.

Holy Basil

There are many species of basil, each with its own distinctive flavour. Sweet basil (*Ocimum basilicum)* is common in gardens and on windowsills and a popular culinary herb because of its use in Italian pasta dishes and pizzas, as well as its winning combination with tomatoes and mozzarella. (Since 2005, 'Genovese' basil has a Protected Designation of Origin (PDO), which means it's not 'Genovese' unless it comes from Genova.)

Basils are all tender plants, some more so than others depending on their place of origin, and are either grown as annuals or brought inside to overwinter. Given suitable lighting conditions they can be productive all year round inside.

Holy Basil, or Tulsi, is *Ocimum tenuiflorum*. It has slightly hairy and serrated leaves with a very pungent flavour. It is cultivated in parts of Asia (including India and Thailand) as a sacred herb, but also has medicinal and culinary uses.

Red and green forms exist, and Holy Basil grows to around 60 cm tall. Plants are easily grown from seeds, which are readily available. Leaves can be brewed into teas, including the traditional Indian Tulsi chai. They are also used in Thai cookery where they are referred to as Thai Holy Basil, to differentiate between them and Thai basil, which is a variety of *O. basilicum.*

Despite its tenderness, Holy Basil is quite a tough, woody plant - its stems have even been used to carve beads for rosaries.

Weeds and Wildings

Here in the UK in the last few years there has been increased interest in foraging - heading out into the local environment to harvest wild ingredients. Foraging books and courses abound, and wild foods are making it onto the menu in fancy restaurants. For some foragers it's just another means of reconnecting with nature and the seasons, with harvests coming and going as the weather dictates. For others it's a way to reduce food bills, or to dine on rarities that would otherwise be unavailable.

All of these motivations will be familiar to anyone who grows unusual edible plants. And with the problems inherent in foraging (legal access to private land, the permissions needed to harvest roots, correct identification of plants, finding places away from pollution, habitat loss and over-collection, etc.) it's not surprising that some gardeners choose to add wild plants to the garden, and harvest them there.

Pignuts

Pignuts (*Conopodium majus*) are small, tuberous roots that form on a plant in the carrot family. Pignuts were once a common sight in the British countryside, and children would have foraged for them as a treat. They're rarer now, mainly due to habitat loss - in the wild they grow in grassland and open woodland. Where once there were abundant clumps, foragers often struggle to find more than a handful of plants.

Also known as earth chestnuts, these tubers are around the size of a walnut and taste a little bit like chestnuts or hazelnuts. They are peeled, and can be eaten raw, boiled or roasted. Some have a radish-like 'hot' aftertaste; it's not entirely clear whether location and soil is the deciding factor, or something else.

Tubers in the wild can be difficult to locate, but in the garden you would expect to find them 15 to 20 centimetres below where the plants are growing - and the tubers themselves are larger when cultivated. To grow your own pignut patch, you'll need to sow seeds in spring. In the UK you can source them from Thomas Etty (see the Resources section for more details).

Dandelions

Deliberately growing dandelions (*Taraxacum officinale*) may earn you some funny looks - they're a well-known weed throughout much of the northern hemisphere. Many gardeners despair of getting them under control as they can regrow from small sections of root if not properly weeded out.

But the dandelion has a long history as a useful plant. Its leaves appear early in spring and are very nutritious (another reason some people prefer wild foods - they are nutrient-dense) and make a good spring tonic. The leaves are eaten young, and before the plant flowers, as they can become too bitter to be palatable (to humans; tortoises seem to like them).

Once the flowers appear, dandelions make a good bee plant. The flowers are edible too, and those pesky tap roots can be roasted and ground for a coffee substitute.

In the unlikely event this wonderful plant hasn't found your garden by itself, it's possible to buy seeds, which are sown in spring. A garden situation makes it easier to blanch the leaves (by excluding light), which makes them far less bitter. The plant can be harvested all summer long, but by early autumn it's time to let it be so that it can recover overwinter for fresh spring harvests.

The Italian red rib dandelion (*Chicorium intybus*) isn't a dandelion at all, it's a chicory. But its leaves have a similar bitter/ sweet flavour profile and the foliage is very eye-catching with its red rib. In urban surroundings it will avoid the wrath of your neighbours who may accuse you of causing weed problems if you encourage true dandelions. Sow seeds in spring, and baby leaf harvests begin around 40 days later. Again, you can cut leaves right through until early autumn, but need to give these perennial plants some recovery time over the winter.

Seeds for both of these plants are easy to find. In the UK try the Organic Gardening Catalogue, Nicky's Nursery and Seeds of Italy.

Alexanders

When I visited Cornwall in April, Alexanders (*Smyrnium olusatrum)* were blooming everywhere in the hedgerows as I drove along the country lanes. Native to Europe and Asia, Alexanders were probably brought to the UK by the Romans - as an edible and medicinal plant.

Alexanders are biennial, and a member of the carrot family - which can make identification in the wild a little tricky. There are poisonous relatives that are similar enough (at various points during the year) to give novice foragers concern.

Growing your own takes that worry away, and gives you access to the plants to dig up roots and to blanch stems and leaves. All parts of the plant are edible, and Alexanders also goes by the name Black Lovage, which gives you a clue about its (celery-like) flavour. In fact, it has been replaced by celery in our gardens and kitchens.

Alexanders stay in leaf throughout the winter, and can be a good source of leafy greens. Most people stick to eating the stems, which are less pungent (particularly after blanching). The roots are used boiled, for example in soup. Even the seeds are edible - as a spicy pepper substitute.

If you want to add this plant to your garden, sow seeds in early spring as they need a little bit of cold to encourage germination. Plants can grow upwards of 90 centimetres tall. UK suppliers include Nicky's Nursery and Chiltern seeds.

Wild strawberries

Humans have been tucking into wild strawberries (*Fragaria vesca)* since the Stone Age. Paradoxically, these 'wild' plants were once widely cultivated, before being largely replaced in the 18th century by the garden strawberry hybrids we see today.

Wild strawberries, like their larger garden cousins, send out lots of runners and are easily propagated that way. A little too easily, perhaps - they make a great groundcover plant, but elsewhere could be considered to be a little on the invasive side. They're easy enough to remove, however, and who wouldn't want a garden carpeted with strawberries?

The fruits are small, but very strongly flavoured, and produced in small batches through the season. In the wild you'd be hard pressed to find more than a few at a time, but in the garden you could easily gather a handful for your breakfast, or to bake into muffins. Wild strawberries are turned into commercial products - they're the gourmet's choice.

'Alpine strawberries' are most likely to be *F. vesca* 'Semperflorens'. They're more discrete, upright plants that bear their fruits on graceful stems above the reach of most slugs. They're also more well-behaved, propagated by seed and division rather than runners. They're very pretty little clumping plants, and wouldn't look out of place in the flower borders.

In both cases, the leaves are also edible and can be used to make a herbal tea. And both types come in two varieties - with the familiar red fruits, but also with white fruits. The white fruits have a more perfumed flavour, and are never bothered by birds. You won't find those in the wild, so if you want them you have to grow your own!

Strawberry seeds are tiny and fiddly to sow. There is often discussion about them being tricky to germinate but I have never found this to be the case. Sow them carefully, be patient (seeds from wilder plants may not germinate as quickly as their more cultivated relatives) and you should be rewarded.

Alpine strawberry seeds are quite readily available, with 'Mignonette' a common variety.

Wild garlic

Ramsons (*Allium ursinum,* also known as Bear's garlic) grow wild in the UK in shady, damp places. At the right time of year their heady garlic scent wafts around on the wind. All parts of the plant are edible, and a forager's favourite. The broad, glossy green leaves can be eaten raw or cooked. The flower buds can be pickled to make something a bit like capers, and the flowers themselves are edible, too. The bulbs are small, and it may not be worth digging them up, but if you to do so they're dug when the plant is dormant in the summer (and so you have to know where they grow, as the leaves die back).

Ramsons do form large stands, and spread very well - under the right conditions they can be invasive. But as an edible perennial that likes a bit of damp and shade, they can be very useful plants. If you want to add them to your garden you can grow them from seed, which needs cold stratification and is therefore sown in autumn. You can also plant bulbs, which are available during the plant's dormant season. Try Nicky's Nursery for seeds.

With their white, star-like flowers appearing from spring to early summer, ramsons could be considered edimentals - if it weren't for their pong!

Samphire

There are two wild plants called 'samphire' that grow in the UK, and they're different species. Rock samphire, *Crithmum maritimum,* is a perennial coastal plant that loves to cling to rocks. The leaves are eaten as an accompaniment to seafood, and the seed pods can be pickled. If you've got a suitable spot in your garden (a rockery, perhaps?) you can sow seed in autumn. Nicky's Nursery is one potential supplier.

Marsh samphire, *Salicornia europea,* is an annual that grows in tidal marshes. It is used in the same way - young leaves can be eaten raw, or lightly cooked. They have a salty tang and are increasingly popular in upscale restaurants. This is the species you would see for sale as a vegetable. To grow your own you'll need a well-drained spot; entertainingly, the recommendation is to water your plants with a saline solution - so they'll need to be kept separate from other plants that won't appreciate salty soil. If you stop harvesting from plants and allow them to flower, they will happily self-seed. I haven't seen seeds for sale, but Victoriana Nursery Gardens supplies plants.

There are other plants with similarly succulent stems that you might like to try. Agretti, *Salsola soda,* is a gourmet vegetable in Italy and Japan. Leaves can be eaten raw, simply braised in olive oil, or boiled and dressed in oil. Germination is patchy, and seed viability is around four months, so you need fresh seed and it's not always easy to come by. Try Seeds of Italy and Real Seeds.

And Okahijiki, Japanese land seaweed, is *Salsola komarovii.* Young leaves are eaten raw, older ones lightly cooked. It can be used for microgreens, and at the 'baby leaf' stage. Again, seed germination may be poor and it's vital to source fresh seed. Try Nicky's Nursery.

Sloes

Sloes grow on buckthorn (*Prunus spinosa)* bushes. They're a popular fruit for foragers, although eaten raw they can be horribly astringent. After being exposed to frost (or the freezer!) they become slightly sweeter, but are usually cooked and made into preserves. The most common use for them in the UK is as a flavouring for Sloe Gin, where they are picked, pricked and packed into a jar with some sugar. After filling the jar with gin it is left to one side until Christmas. The gin-soaked sloes can be eaten, and the sloe gin will get the mid-winter festivities off to a flying start!

Blackthorn tends to be a large tree, but can be kept as a bush in a garden with suitable pruning. It is often used as a hedging plant, and its thorns add an extra layer of protection from intruders. Plant one and you'll be rewarded with clouds of white flowers in April and May, which are also popular with bees and beneficial insects. Sloes are picked in autumn.

Blackthorn has a tendency to send out suckers, which is fine where there are grazing animals to keep them under control; in a garden setting you may want to confine your bush to a container.

Bare-root blackthorn plants are readily available from hedging suppliers. If you want just one or two, pot-grown plants, try Victoriana Nursery Gardens.

Garlic Mustard

Garlic mustard, Jack-by-the-hedge (*Alliaria petiolata*) likes dappled shade. It has a garlic flavour and leaves can be eaten raw or cooked. Its flowers are also edible, and it's worth trying flower shoots cooked like sprouting broccoli. It's an easily recognised plant, and a popular choice with foragers.

An annual plant, garlic mustard flowers from spring through to midsummer, and is good for wildlife. If you wanted to try the roots, they are said to make a good substitute for horseradish.

Seeds are sown in spring, or in autumn. UK suppliers include the Organic Gardening Catalogue, Nicky's Nursery and Chiltern Seeds.

Bucks Horn Plantain

Bucks Horn Plantain, *Plantago coronopus,* has some lovely common names. It's also known as Minutina, Herba Stella and Capuchin's Beard. It has crunchy leaves with a herby flavour that can be added to salads when they're young and are used as a garnish. Leaves can be cooked, and in times past they have been turned into a jelly, much like mint jelly, and used as a condiment for roasted meats. The flowers are also edible.

Happy with maritime exposure, Bucks Horn Plantain is also relatively hardy. A biennial, it can be grown as an annual where the climate isn't conducive, with plants being started indoors where the season is short.

Sow in spring for leaf harvests through to midsummer. Plants will then flower and set seed - save the seed and sow in autumn for crops through to midwinter (although they may benefit from protection in colder areas).

I have seen seeds on offer at Nicky's Nursery and the Organic Gardening Catalogue.

CHAPTER FOUR

Resources

Dangers and Warnings
Native v non-native

There are several topics that divide gardeners - whether you should dig your patch, or not. Whether you should be organic or not. Whether native plants are better for garden ecosystems or not. It's obviously more comfortable to be on one side of the fence, rather than perched on top, but things are rarely that simple.

The argument for native plants is that they are better for local wildlife, and while it's true that some species need a particular species (or a small number of species), most aren't actually that fussy. A scientific study carried out here in the UK proved that there are plants, and garden features, that encourage wildlife into your garden - but they're not often what you think. The project was entertainingly documented in 'No More Nettles', by Ken Thompson, which is well worth a read if you really want a wildlife friendly garden.

As we saw at the beginning of the book, many of the edible species we rely on have travelled a long way to get onto our dinner tables - even if it happened so long ago that we can't imagine life without them. Here in the UK a 'native' diet would be particularly tricky, as our separation from mainland Europe during the last ice age means we missed out on having lots of tasty native species.

And how do you define native, anyway? How far back into the past does a species have to arrived before it can be classed as a native? Or are we limiting ourselves to plants which evolved in our local area, in which case nearly all of us are going to get very hungry indeed.

The waters get even muddier, because plants move. We think they sit idly by, waiting for life to come to them, but in actual fact they are always doing their best to expand their territories. They send seeds off on the wind, or stuck to animals, in search of pastures new. And globalisation means that they can hitch a ride with us - on travellers' clothing, or freight packaging, or in water used as ballast or a hundred other things we move around the globe.

In short, there's a place for native plants in gardens, but it's not the veg patch. That being said, we do have to be careful not to introduce botanical thugs....

Invasive plants

Outside of its natural habitat, any species has the potential to become invasive - a pest. It's to do with ecological balance and the lack of predators. Here in the UK we have several problem species, including rhododendrons, Himalayan balsam and Japanese knotweed that were all introduced as ornamental plants. While it's still possible to add a rhododendron to your garden if you have the right soil, the other two are classed as noxious weeds and there are laws governing their removal and disposal.

Invasive plants out-compete species that were already there, and in doing so change the entire ecosystem. Removing them, for commercial reasons or to protect habitats, costs a fortune and is quite often a losing battle - in some places control is the aim, rather than complete eradication.

There are sometimes calls for us to eat our way through our invasive species - the idea being that we become their predator and control the population that way. But while dedicated foragers can be relied upon to selectively remove invasive plants (more on that, later), the general public would need a good deal of education before being able to make a positive impact.

Gardeners normally only have to deal with invasive plants on a smaller scale. We all know of plants that can be tricky to remove from a garden once they've settled in - Jerusalem artichokes regenerate from the smallest tuber (as do Chinese artichokes), mint is thuggish in most climates and positively invasive in others. Wild strawberries send out runners at the rate of knots, but at least they're reasonably easy to pull up.

Our responsibility is to ensure that the plants we encourage in our gardens, stay in our gardens, and are not allowed to escape into our local environment. Do your homework (in the UK, DEFRA and Plantlife (http://www.plantlife.org.uk) are good starting points), keep an eye on your plants and always dispose of potentially problematic plant waste responsibly.

Invasive species are one reason why so many countries have...

Import restrictions

The websites and catalogues of seed companies explain carefully the countries to which they will send seeds and plants. They won't all ship everywhere, and some of that is down to economic factors. But a lot of it is down to import and export restrictions. Within the EU there are very few; between the EU and other countries in the world there are plenty. The USA and Australia are notoriously tough on what's allowed across their borders.

And that makes perfect sense - we don't want invasive plants being dispersed across the globe with no controls (although, as previously discussed, it's not entirely possible to stop them). We also don't want to spread the pests and diseases that affect plants, particularly crop species, and that is also a very real threat. And that's one reason why it's easier to import seeds than 'live' plant material.

One of the plant families with the tightest restrictions is the Solanums - tomatoes, peppers, potatoes, aubergines - lots of tasty plants there. When goji berries became popular in the UK a few years ago, and started to be imported in larger numbers, there were concerns that they could be a vector for all kinds of nasty diseases to which other Solanums would be vulnerable. Fortunately now they are mainly grown and despatched from within the EU.

My point here is that, while it's easy to think there's no harm in importing a few seeds or plants, there could well be. Internet swaps and purchases often circumvent the tough controls seed companies are forced to adhere to (phytosanitary certificates, and more). Be a good citizen and know what's allowed in your country, and what isn't, and why. Packages containing contraband could be stopped entering or leaving the country, so be careful what you swap and with whom.

Correct identification and allergies, etc.

So you've done your research, and sourced your seeds and plants, and planted them and nurtured them and it's finally time to harvest them. It's also time to double-check that your plant is everything you expected.

People make mistakes. Sometimes they say something is edible, when it isn't (and vice versa). Science moves on, and some of the plants that were considered edible in times past are now considered to be less so - comfrey being a prime example. It's not exactly poisonous, but it's not something most people consider safe to eat now. When you're growing unusual edibles it pays to keep an ear to the ground and keep re-evaluating what's on your "must try" list.

People make mistakes. Bulbs get mixed up, plants can be wrongly labelled, seeds can be mixed up or contaminated with other species. If you've sown seeds, or watched a plant die back right to the ground and spring back to life - are you *sure* that what has come up is what you expected? Wherever possible, source your plants and seeds from reputable suppliers.

Unusual edibles aren't always straightforward. Common or garden varieties have been bred so that any noxious chemicals and wayward tendencies are long gone. Many slightly wilder plants need to be prepared properly before they are edible. Proper Preparation Prevents Poisoning!

And there are always allergies to be taken into consideration with novel foods - whether you've grown them or not. Try them in small amounts at first, and if there's even the slightest doubt about identification then keep some on hand for later analysis in case you run into problems. In March 2012 there were several cases of poisoning among the British Chinese population, with victims having eaten daffodils wrongly identified as Chinese chives (http://www.bbc.co.uk/news/uk-england-bristol-17233766).

In the safety of your own garden, you (should) know what's planted where - and that's a big help. But when you venture outside, it's a different story....

Wild harvesting

Whether you're heading out on a foraging trip to find plants to munch on, or to introduce into the garden, there are some things you should bear in mind - beyond ensuring you have correctly identified your plants. I'm going to hand you over to Carl Legge (www.carllegge.com), so that he can walk you through his Sustainable Foraging Guidelines.

There are three areas in which you need to act sustainably when foraging:

Your environment

Your community

Yourself

Guidelines for your Environment

Leave produce for animals to feed on, for the plant to propagate itself and for it to nourish its patch. Leave some produce on each plant you pick from.

Only take what you'll be able to use.

If you can, sow seeds or scatter the fruit pips that you have left over from processing so that you help plants propagate.

Only take plants that are not on protected or endangered lists.

Learn how to harvest plants without damaging them.

Guidelines for your Community

Leave some produce for others to enjoy, to look at and to collect.

Be generous with your advice & assistance to others so you encourage them to look after your shared environment.

Guidelines for Yourself

Only take what you can comfortably process or store for later processing.

Use appropriate precautions when collecting. Gloves can be useful for protecting against stings and thorns. A brimmed hat can help you avoid poking yourself in the eyes with branches.

Stay within the law: have permission or a legal right for where you are and what you want to pick.

Be aware of pollution issues as they might affect the things you want to pick.

Internet etiquette

It's easy to see the internet as a scary world filled with trolls and scammers and dangerous to good old, regular folk. It's also easy to see it as an entirely benign, virtual, world in which no harm can come to you. Neither extreme is true. I like to think of the internet as a big city, where there are some lovely folks, some you'd rather not know, and some who are out to trick you. There are friendly places, dodgy places and places where angels fear to tread.

Gardeners and unusual edibles fanatics who hang out online tend to be lovely, friendly and generous people. They give their time (and seeds) merely to help out others. They have all encountered people who were only after freebies, and disappeared without a trace once they had them. Don't be one of them, it's not nice.

You may have noticed that not all of the plants mentioned in the book (particularly if they were mentioned by one of the interviewees) have been associated with their scientific (binomial, or Latin) name. That may not seem very helpful - you can't just nip out and find seeds for it and plant it in your garden. You can't be immediately sure you've got the right plant. But it was a deliberate choice on my part; this book isn't a gardening manual. It's not intended to give you all the answers, a garden plan and a shopping list. I want you to begin your own unusual edibles journey, not follow in our footsteps.

That said, almost all of the people mentioned in the book have a significant online presence - whether it's a blog or a Twitter account or a Facebook page. They are all lovely, friendly, people who will happily answer your questions if you seek them out and ask them *nicely*. They may have seeds to share you with you; if you don't have anything to swap then remember to offer to cover postage costs - some people send out a lot of plant material, and the costs to them soon add up.

Do not expect anyone overseas to send you anything for which the import or export is restricted.

You may find that the only person with the plant you're desperately trying to track down doesn't speak your language. Google Translate is your friend, up to a certain point. Translate your email before you send it - don't expect a stranger to read emails in a language they can't understand.

There are lots of internet forums related to gardening and permaculture and all kinds of things that may have relevant information and may organise seed swaps that you want to join. Don't just barge in and request or demand seeds - it's rude. Think of a forum as a coffee morning where everyone else knows everyone, and you're a stranger. There are plenty of people who will welcome you and be interested in what you have to say, and they may choose to help you out - but not if you have bad manners.

Books

'Lost Crops of the Incas: Little-Known Plants of the Andes with Promise for Worldwide Cultivation'. The National Academies Press, 1989. Print copies are available (although sometimes expensive), but a free PDF copy can be downloaded from http://www.nap.edu/catalog.php?record_id=1398.

'The Alternative Kitchen Garden: An A to Z'. Emma Cooper, Permanent Publications, 2009.

'The Earth Knows My Name: Food, Culture, and Sustainability in the Gardens of Ethnic America'. Patricia Klindienst, Beacon Press, 2007.

'Breed Your Own Vegetable Varieties: The Gardener's and Farmers Guide to Plant Breeding and Seed Saving'. Carol Deppe, Chelsea Green, 1990.

'Cornucopia II: A Source Book of Edible Plants'. Stephen Facciola, Kampong Publications, 1998.

'Plants for a Future: Edible and Useful Plants for a Healthier World'. Ken Fern, Permanent Publications, 1997.

'Oriental Vegetables'. Joy Larkcom, Frances Lincoln, 2007.

'Asian Vegetables: A Guide to Growing Fruit, Vegetables and Spices from the Indian Subcontinent'. Sally Cunningham, Eco-Logic Books, 2009.

'Growing Unusual Vegetables: Weird and Wonderful Vegetables and How to Grow Them'. Simon Hickmott, Eco-Logic Books, 2004.

'Flora Britannica'. Richard Mabey, Chatto & Windus, 1996.

'A Taste of the Unexpected'. Mark Diacono, Quadrille Publishing Ltd, 2010.

'The Kitchen Gardens at Heligan: Lost Gardening Principles Rediscovered'. Tom Petherick and Melanie Eclare, W&N, 2006.

'Perennial Vegetables'. Eric Toensmeier, Chelsea Green, 2007.

'How to Grow Perennial Vegetables: Low-maintenance, Low-impact Vegetable Gardening'. Martin Crawford, Green Books, 2012.

'Edible Forest Gardens'. David Jacke and Eric Toensmeier, Chelsea Green, 2005.

'Just Vegetating: A Memoir'. Joy Larkcom, Frances Lincoln, 2012.

'The Lost Art of Potato Breeding'. Rebsie Fairholm, Skylight Press, 2014.

'Around the Word in 80 Plants'. Stephen Barstow, Permanent Publications, 2014.

Websites

http://emmacooper.org
My website, home to my blog and the Alternative Kitchen Garden
podcast as well as more information about my books.

http://www.japanfarmersmarkets.com
Joan Lambert Bailey's blog about vegetable growing in Japan and local
farmer's markets.

http://alanbishop.proboards.com
The Homegrown Goodness forum.

http://www.pfaf.org
The Plants for a Future online database, considerably updated from the
book.

http://myfolia.com
A social media hangout for gardeners.

http://www.sowingnewseeds.org.uk
Garden Organic's project to enable allotment holders, schools and
community groups in the Midlands to grow exotic crops not traditionally
grown in the UK.

http://subsistencepatternfoodgarden.blogspot.com
Mike Hannon's online home.

http://toads.wordpress.com
Søren Holt's stories of seed-saving in Denmark.

http://oca-testbed.blogspot.co.uk
Ian Pearson's record of his oca growing experiments, and more.

http://vegetablevagabond.blogspot.com

Kate Flint, sowing seeds and putting down roots in Tasmania.

http://www.risc.org.uk/gardens
The RISC garden.

http://radix4roots.blogspot.co.uk
Rooting around with Owen Smith.

http://carllegge.com
Carl Legge's home cooked goodness.

Suppliers

There is not enough space here to list every single seed and plant supplier, even in the UK. Many are now adding heritage or unusual varieties to their listings, and it's worth pouring over the glossy catalogues that fall through the letterbox every season. But I am concentrating here on the smaller nurseries, or those dedicated to unusual plants, of which I am aware. I have also tried to include the contact details of companies mentioned elsewhere in the book.

Not all of these suppliers have nurseries and shops that are open to the public, and some only open by arrangement. Please check the websites for further details before making a special trip.

UK

Agroforestry Research Trust

A non-profit organisation that researches temperate agroforestry and perennial crops. Plants and seeds are available via mail order. International seed sales are possible, but not to the US or Canada and the website notes the strict quarantine requirements of Australia.

A.R.T. 46 Hunters Moon, Dartington, Totnes, TQ9 6JT

Website: http://www.agroforestry.co.uk

Email: mail@agroforestry.co.uk

Avon Bulbs

A specialist, family-run, nursery offering a range of unusual and rare bulbs in the UK and EU.

Avon Bulbs, Burnt House Farm, Mid Lambrook, South Petherton, Somerset, TA13 5HE

Website: http://www.avonbulbs.co.uk

Email: info@avonbulbs.co.uk

Chiltern Seeds

'Grow something new from seed' is the company motto, and they have an extensive range of seeds available, with vegetable seeds now separated into their 'Veg Book' printed catalogue. International orders are accepted.

Chiltern Seeds, Bortree Stile, Ulverston, Cumbria, LA12 7PB

Website: http://www.chilternseeds.co.uk

Email: info@chilternseeds.co.uk

Twitter: @chilternseeds

CN Seeds

Independent supplier and breeder of salad, baby leaf, herb, vegetable and flower seeds.

CN Seeds Ltd. Pymoor, Ely, Cambridgeshire , CB6 2ED

Website: http://www.cnseeds.co.uk

Email: info@cnseeds.co.uk

Cool Temperate Nursery

'Plants and services for a sustainable world', mainly fruit trees and nitrogen-fixing species for forest gardens, plus *Hablitzia tamnoides*.

Cool Temperate Nursery, 45 Stamford Street, Awsworth, Notts, NG16 2QL

Website: http://www.cooltemperate.co.uk

Email: phil.corbett@cooltemperate.co.uk

Crûg Farm Plants

Introducing new and wondrous plants from our annual sorties to remote corners of the globe.

Crûg Farm Plants, Griffith's Crossing, Caernarfon, Gwynedd, LL55 1TU

Website: http://crug-farm.co.uk

Email: mailorder@crug-farm.co.uk

Edulis

Growers of rare plants, including fruit, herbs and perennial vegetables.

Edulis, 1 Flowers Piece, Ashampstead, Reading, RG8 8SG

Website: http://www.edulis.co.uk

Email: info@edulis.co.uk

Heritage Seed Library (Garden Organic)

A members-only seed catalogue for heritage vegetables. Selections vary from year to year, and include unusual varieties collected via the Sowing New Seeds project. International members are accepted, but if you are outside the EU it is your responsibility to check whether phytosanitary certificates are required (the implication being that they cannot be provided).

Garden Organic, Ryton, Coventry, Warwickshire, United Kingdom, CV8 3LG

Website: http://www.gardenorganic.org.uk/heritage

Email: hsl@gardenorganic.org.uk

Jekka's Herb Farm

An award-winning organic nursery specialising in herbs, with over 650 varieties in their collection. Culinary, aromatic, decorative and medicinal herbs are all represented. Now only sells seeds via mail order, but plants are available to buy from the nursery on special open days.

Jekka's Herb Farm, Rose Cottage, Shellards Lane, Alveston, Bristol, BS35 3SY

Website: http://www.jekkasherbfarm.com

Email: sales@jekkasherbfarm.com

Jungle Seeds

Nursery specialising in 'supplying tropical seeds, tropical tubers/rhizomes and tropical plants'. They have an expanding vegetable seed collection as well as tropical fruit plants.

JungleSeeds&Gardens, PO Box 45, Watlington, SPDO, Oxon, OX49 5YR

Website: http://www.jungleseeds.co.uk

Email: contactjungle@jungleseeds.co.uk

Twitter: @JungleSeedsUK

Kore Wild Fruit Nursery

A small-scale nursery specialising in plants that produce edible fruit, from all over the world.

Kore Wild Fruit Nursery, Warren Fields Farm, Trellech, Monmouth, Gwent, NP25 4PQ

Website: http://www.korewildfruitnursery.co.uk

Email: info@korewildfruitnursery.co.uk

Nicky's Nursery

Online company offering a large range of vegetable, oriental, baby veg, tomato, chilli seeds, herb, tree, wildflower and flower garden seeds.

Nicky's Nursery, Fairfield Road, Broadstairs, Kent, CT10 2JU

Website: http://www.nickys-nursery.co.uk

Email: seeds@nickys-nursery.co.uk

The Organic Gardening Catalogue

Organic seeds for vegetables, heritage and modern varieties, herbs, flowers and green manures.

The Organic Gardening Catalogue, Riverdene Business Park, Molesey Road, Hersham, Surrey, KT12 4RG

Website: http://www.organiccatalogue.com

Organic Plants

A large range of mail order vegetable plants, delivered at the right time for planting and propagated in peat-free growing media. Their range also includes seed potatoes and vegetable seeds, but the jewels in the crown are a range of grafted vegetables (aubergines, peppers, cucumbers and tomatoes) and heritage tomato plants produced in conjunction with the Heritage Seed Library.

Delfland Nurseries Limited, Benwick Road, Doddington, March, Cambs, PE15 0TU

Website: http://www.organicplants.co.uk

Email: info@organicplants.co.uk

Twitter: @organicplantsuk

Poyntzfield Herb Nursery

400 varieties of herbs for sale via the nursery or mail order, including international delivery.

Poyntzfield Herb Nursery, Black Isle, By Dingwall, IV7 8LX, Ross & Cromarty, Scotland

Website: http://www.poyntzfieldherbs.co.uk

Email: info@poyntzfieldherbs.co.uk

Real Seed Catalogue

Suppliers of open-pollinated vegetable and herb seeds and varieties guaranteed to grow in the British climate. Their collection includes 'Fat Baby' achocha and the exploding cucumber, a number of oca varieties and yacón, although unusual crops usually have limited availability.

Real Seeds, PO Box 18, Newport near Fishguard, Pembrokeshire, SA65 0AA

Website: http://realseeds.co.uk

Email: info@realseeds.co.uk

Sea Spring Seeds

Plant-hunters and breeders, always on the lookout for new and exceptional varieties.

Sea Spring Farm, West Bexington, Dorchester, West Dorset, DT2 9DD

Website: http://www.seaspringseeds.co.uk

Email: info@seaspringseeds.co.uk

Seeds of Italy

Their 'Golden Line' contains unusual items such as chickpeas and lentils, rice and other grains, peanuts and living pet foods. Check the details for each individual catalogue item, as some cannot be shipped outside the UK.

Seeds of Italy Ltd, A1 Phoenix Industrial Estate, Rosslyn Crescent, Harrow, HA1 2SP

Website: http://www.seedsofitaly.com

Email: grow@italianingredients.com

Twitter: @FranchiSeedsUK

Simpson's Seeds

Specialists in tomatoes, capsicums, cucumbers, melons and other greenhouse crops.

Simpson's Seeds, The Walled Garden Nursery , Horningsham, Warminster, BA12 7NQ

Website: http://www.simpsonsseeds.co.uk

Email: sales@simpsonsseeds.co.uk

Suffolk Herbs

An extensive range of herb seeds, together with oriental and unusual vegetables. Overseas orders are accepted, request a catalogue for more details.

Suffolk Herbs, Monks Farm, Coggeshall Road, Kelvedon, Essex, CO5 9PG

Website: http://www.kingsseeds.com

Email: info@kingsseeds.com

Thomas Etty Esq.

Suppliers of 'heritage seeds and bulbs for the period garden', including a large selection of heritage vegetable varieties.

Thomas Etty Esq. Seedsman's Cottage, Puddlebridge, Horton, Ilminster, Somerset, TA19 9RL

Website: http://thomasetty.co.uk

Email: sales@thomasetty.co.uk

Twitter: @thomasetty

Tozer Seeds

The UK's largest independent vegetable seeds breeder.

Tozer Seeds Ltd, Pyports, Downside Bridge Road, Cobham, Surrey, KT11 3EH

Website: http://www.tozerseeds.com

Email: sales@tozerseeds.com

Tropical Fruit and Veg

Supplies seeds of tropical fruit and vegetable plants from around the world.

Website: http://tropicalfruitandveg.com

Twitter: @tropicalfnv

Victoriana Nursery Gardens

Friendly supplier of quality seeds and plants for the discerning gardener. A family business with tradition.

Victoriana Nursery Gardens, Challock, Nr Ashford, Kent, TN25 4DG

Website: http://www.victoriananursery.co.uk

Email: sales@victoriananursery.co.uk

Europe

Arche Noah

For more than 20 years ARCHE NOAH and its 10,000 members have been preserving and cultivating endangered vegetable, fruit and grain diversity.

Website: https://www.arche-noah.at

Association Kokopelli

A non-profit organisation based in France and dedicated to preservation and dissemination of ancient vegetable varieties.

Website: http://www.terredesemences.com

US website: http://www.kokopelli-seed-foundation.com

Email: contactus@organicseedsonline.com

B&T World Seeds

Aims to be the world's most extensive commercial seed catalogue, specialising in rare and exotic seeds. Ships internationally.

B & T World Seeds, Paguigan, 34210 Aigues-Vives, France

Website: http://b-and-t-world-seeds.com

Email: heather@b-and-t-world-seeds.com

Twitter: @Matthew_Sleigh

Runåbergs Fröer

Runåbergs seeds, Kans Torp 147, S-444 93 Spekeröd, Sweden

Website: http://www.runabergsfroer.se

US & Canada

Adaptive Seeds

Artisan quality, public domain, open-pollinated seeds, grown without the use of synthetic chemicals and with ecologically mindful methods. Their catalog is full of robust productive varieties as well as rare adaptive gems.

Adaptive Seeds, 25079 Brush Creek Rd, Sweet Home, OR 97386, USA

Website: http://www.adaptiveseeds.com

Email: adaptiveseeds@gmail.com

Baker Creek Heirloom Seeds

Suppliers of 1400 open-pollinated and GMO-free heirloom seed varieties.

Baker Creek Heirloom Seed Co. 2278 Baker Creek Road, Mansfield, MO 65704, USA

Website: http://www.rareseeds.com

Email: seeds@rareseeds.com

Horizon Herbs

Certified organic herb seeds, vegetable seeds and plants. Welcomes international seed orders

Horizon Herbs, LLC. PO Box 69, Williams, OR 97544, USA

Website: https://www.horizonherbs.com

Email: hhcustserv@HorizonHerbs.com

Tater-Mater Seeds

A very small operation distributing seeds for the tomato and potato seed (yes, seed, not seed potatoes) varieties developed by Tom Wagner. International shipping is a possibility.

Tater-Mater Seeds, PO Box 16085, Seattle, WA 98116, USA

Website: http://tatermaterseeds.com/shop

Richters

Herb specialists, supplying both seeds and plants to the US & Canada. Seeds only internationally. Their new Seed Zoo™ collection is still expanding, with rare and endangered food plants from around the world.

Richters Herbs, 357 Highway 47, Goodwood, ON, L0C 1A0, Canada

Website: http://www.richters.com

Twitter: @richtersherbs

Seeds of Change

Supply an extensive range of organically-grown vegetable, flower, herb and cover crop seeds.

Seeds of Change, P.O. Box 4908, Rancho Dominguez, CA 90224, USA

Website: http://www.seedsofchange.com

Twitter: @SeedsofChange

Seed Savers Exchange

A non-profit membership organisation dedicated to saving and sharing heirloom seeds. Overseas memberships are available.

Seeds of Change, 3094 North Winn Road, Decorah, Iowa 52101, USA

Website: http://www.seedsavers.org

Twitter: @Seedsaversx

Thank you for reading my book. If you enjoyed it, would you take a moment to leave me a review?

Many thanks

Emma Cooper

11968762R00096

Printed in Great Britain
by Amazon.co.uk, Ltd.,
Marston Gate.